Cambridge Elements

Elements of Christianity and Science
edited by
Andrew Davison
University of Cambridge

THOMISM AND THE NATURAL SCIENCES

Ignacio Silva
Universidad Austral

CAMBRIDGE
UNIVERSITY PRESS

Shaftesbury Road, Cambridge CB2 8EA, United Kingdom

One Liberty Plaza, 20th Floor, New York, NY 10006, USA

477 Williamstown Road, Port Melbourne, VIC 3207, Australia

314–321, 3rd Floor, Plot 3, Splendor Forum, Jasola District Centre, New Delhi – 110025, India

103 Penang Road, #05–06/07, Visioncrest Commercial, Singapore 238467

Cambridge University Press is part of Cambridge University Press & Assessment, a department of the University of Cambridge.

We share the University's mission to contribute to society through the pursuit of education, learning and research at the highest international levels of excellence.

www.cambridge.org
Information on this title: www.cambridge.org/9781009547970

DOI: 10.1017/9781009429825

© Ignacio Silva 2025

This publication is in copyright. Subject to statutory exception and to the provisions of relevant collective licensing agreements, no reproduction of any part may take place without the written permission of Cambridge University Press & Assessment.

When citing this work, please include a reference to the DOI 10.1017/9781009429825

First published 2025

A catalogue record for this publication is available from the British Library

ISBN 978-1-009-54797-0 Hardback
ISBN 978-1-009-42980-1 Paperback
ISSN 2634-3460 (online)
ISSN 2634-3452 (print)

Cambridge University Press & Assessment has no responsibility for the persistence or accuracy of URLs for external or third-party internet websites referred to in this publication and does not guarantee that any content on such websites is, or will remain, accurate or appropriate.

For EU product safety concerns, contact us at Calle de José Abascal, 56, 1°, 28003 Madrid, Spain, or email eugpsr@cambridge.org

Thomism and the Natural Sciences

Elements of Christianity and Science

DOI: 10.1017/9781009429825
First published online: September 2025

Ignacio Silva
Universidad Austral

Author for correspondence: Ignacio Silva, iasilva@austral.edu.ar

Abstract: This Element argues for a novel approach to the sciences within Thomism, namely, science-engaged Thomism, which, aligned with the recent science-engaged theology movement, asks theological and metaphysical questions that require the input of the natural sciences. Recent developments within Thomism show a new approach to the natural sciences, and, thus, the proposal is to encourage more of this discourse by portraying the differences between contemporary and past Thomism. Still, even if it takes a novel approach, science-engaged Thomism relies on a tradition of thought that possesses a vast arsenal of metaphysical tools. Thus, after presenting this approach and a concise introduction to some basic notions of Thomistic metaphysics, the Element reviews some theological and philosophical questions and their relation to the natural sciences: issues about creation, cosmology, and astrobiology, divine involvement in evolutionary biology, providence and indeterministic quantum processes, and some ideas for further development at the end.

Keywords: Thomism, Science and Theology, Thomism and Science, Thomas Aquinas, Science-Engaged Theology

© Ignacio Silva 2025

ISBNs: 9781009547970 (HB), 9781009429801 (PB), 9781009429825 (OC)
ISSNs: 2634-3460 (online), 2634-3452 (print)

Contents

1	Introduction	1
2	Some Preliminary Definitions	5
3	Quantum Mechanics	15
4	Cosmology	25
5	Evolutionary Biology	34
6	Further Developments	51
7	Conclusion	60
	List of Abbreviations of Thomas Aquinas' Works	62
	References	63

1 Introduction

Thomas Aquinas, one of the greatest theological minds, started in the thirteenth century what might be one of the longest intellectual traditions in philosophical and theological history, namely, Thomism. This Element will be devoted to showing how this tradition has of late engaged with the natural sciences. I will suggest that there is at hand a new methodology, which I called 'science-engaged Thomism', that can be conceived in broader terms as aligned with the recent science-engaged theology movement, asking theological questions that require the input of the natural sciences. Still, science-engaged Thomism relies on a tradition of thought that possesses a vast arsenal of metaphysical tools with which to consider the natural sciences and address contemporary questions that arise therefrom. As such, recent, and not so recent, developments have modified, reinterpreted, or reformulated, when necessary, Thomistic notions as they were informed by the natural sciences.

Thomas Aquinas' philosophical and theological production is vast, and this is not the place to comment on it. Suffice it to say that he wrote the *Summa Contra Gentiles*, the *Summa Theologiae*, biblical commentaries, commentaries on Aristotle and on Peter Lombard's *Sentences*, as well as many other commentaries to different Neo-Platonic works, in addition to numerous opuscules, letters, and other minor writings. Due to his adoption of Aristotelian ideas, Aquinas found himself in the middle of two opposing sides: the philosophers who read Aristotle following some Arabic commentators such as Ibn-Rushd (or Averroes, as he was known then), and the theologians who claimed that Aristotelian philosophy implied the falsity of several theological claims. Throughout his life, he placed his thought between these two positions, arguing that Aristotelian philosophy was key to understanding the contents of faith.

1.1 What Is Thomism?

The history of Thomism as a school of thought is vast and long, and, again, I will not attempt to present one here.[1] Interestingly, one cannot really claim that Thomas left disciples during his life. In fact, it took several decades for his ideas to take hold in the minds of scholars. The epithet 'Thomist' was used from the fourteenth century onwards, first to distinguish those who defended Aquinas' doctrines against other positions, such as the Scotists or, later, the Molinists. Then, the label came to mean something broader as those who followed Aquinas' ideas in one way or another. Leonard Kennedy has produced

---

[1] For a short history of early Thomism up to the eighteenth century, see Fabro 2022.

a catalogue of Thomists from the late thirteenth century onwards until the nineteenth century, listing 2034 scholars over six centuries.[2]

Romanus Cessario has claimed, however, that 'there are no universally agreed criteria for answering the question: Who is a Thomist?'[3] Still, the most widely used definition for is that of James Weisheipl, OP (1923–1984). For him, Thomism is 'a theological and philosophical movement that begins in the thirteenth century, and embodies a systematic attempt to understand and develop the basic principles and conclusions of St Thomas Aquinas in order to relate them to the problems and needs of each generation'.[4] That is, Thomism is a historical movement and tradition that does not merely repeat Aquinas' ideas, but rather develops Aquinas' key notions as to face the philosophical and theological problems of the day. Thus, it started with Thomas Aquinas, grew through the fourteenth century, became prominent in the following centuries, particularly through the Counter-Reformation, and continued to expand and flourish until today.

Interestingly, each era has engaged with Aquinas' ideas differently. So, for instance, the early Thomists read more eagerly Aquinas' *Commentary on the Sentences*, whereas both *Summae* were more influential throughout the sixteenth century until the mid twentieth century. Today, scholars are moving beyond the *Summae* and offering due attention to his other philosophical and theological works.[5]

Almost every Thomist would agree to some basic philosophical principles. These include, for a start, metaphysical realism, due to the emphasis given to the act of being or existence. From this, the reality of creation, followed by the possibility of knowing, though imperfectly, the divine nature from its works, and the discourse about it in analogical terms. In addition, within the philosophy of nature, a Thomist would hold that natural things are hylomorphically composed, human beings having a special hylomorphic composition due to their *intellectual* soul.

Throughout its history, Thomism received a great deal of Pontifical support, ever since John XXII canonised Aquinas about fifty years after his death. Mandates and commendations to study Aquinas are present in the Code of Canon Law (Can. 252, §3) and in several nineteenth- and twentieth-century Papal encyclicals,[6] particularly Pope Leo XIII's 1879 encyclical, *Aeterni Patris*. In this letter, Pope Leo stated a straightforward mandate to study the work of Thomas Aquinas in every Catholic institution around the globe, calling all Catholic philosophers and theologians to restore Christian Philosophy in the

---

[2] Kennedy 1987.   [3] Cessario 2003, 20.   [4] Weisheipl 1967, 126.   [5] See Cessario 2003, 11.
[6] Once again, Fabro's volume is an excellent resource.

spirit of the thought of Aquinas. This mandate started what is known as Neo-Thomism, a movement that lasted until the mid twentieth century and that produced a plethora of volumes that attempted to systematise the thought of Thomas Aquinas in direct engagement with then-contemporary philosophical ideas.[7] These volumes were used worldwide well into the second half of the century. An important example for us is that of the Catholic University of Leuven, which, following the papal mandate, decided to open a Thomistic Philosophy Chair. The call for applicants explicitly requested the chairholder to be 'both a learned scholastic and a modern man ... and having followed the development of the sciences, psycho-physics, cell microscopy'.[8] The Catholic Belgian priest Désiré Mercier (1851–1926), later the influential Cardinal Mercier, was selected for it, holding it until 1905. During his tenure, he created the Higher Institute of Philosophy, a beacon of Thomist philosophy, in which scholars were encouraged to engage with the modern sciences, in particular through a laboratory for experimental psychology.

Many have argued that after the Second Vatican Council (1962–1965), Thomism was a dying tradition.[9] Others, however, offer a different assessment. Romanus Cessario, OP, has suggested Thomism remains active in both secular and religious circles.[10] Corroborating this point is the fact, of particular interest to us, that the thought of Thomas Aquinas has seen a revival in the studies of science and theology.

Regarding the natural sciences, there is no clear agreement on how to interpret their results among Thomist. There are at least two main streams of thought, namely, that of Jacques Maritain (1882–1973) and that of the so-called River Forest Thomism, with authors such as Charles de Koninck (1906–1965), James Weisheipl (1923–1984), William Wallace (1918–2015), and Benedict Ashley (1915–2013).[11] These two streams disagreed most basically on the value of the natural sciences in knowing nature and advancing the philosophical and theological enterprise. For Maritain, the natural sciences, which are truly distinct from the philosophy of nature, reach knowledge of nature but only at the observable and measurable level to formulate laws of the regularities observed, while the philosophy of nature reaches nature's essence, that is, it penetrates the nature of its object of study.[12] For River Forest Thomism, on the contrary, the natural sciences are an intrinsic part of the philosophy of nature, meaning that they reach knowledge of the very nature of things. In affirming this, River Forest Thomism stresses the idea that Thomist metaphysics must be

---

[7] See Elders 2020, 13.   [8] Van Riel 2022.   [9] See Rahner 1983, 4.
[10] Cessario 2022, 12. Also, Torrell 2003; Hudson 1992.
[11] See Reese 2024 for a recent analysis of this school within Thomism.
[12] See Maritain 1959, 178–180.

preceded by a study of the natural sciences interpreted under the light of Aristotelian philosophy.[13] Building on this tradition, I will suggest constructing what I have termed in the past as science-engaged Thomism, that is, a Thomism, both philosophical and theological, that is actively and positively engaged with the natural sciences. The main point will be that this active and positive engagement was the attitude that Thomas Aquinas had towards the knowledge of the natural world of his time, so that, despite the formal difference between that knowledge and the natural sciences today, a Thomist could be inspired by Aquinas' own example in doing philosophical and theological work.

In the next section I will present this strategy in depth together with some basic Thomistic metaphysics of nature and of God, creation and providential action in particular, as ground on which to build the presentation of the subsequent sections. Basically, I will offer a simple analysis of the underlying philosophical resources brought from Aristotelian philosophy of nature in terms of the four classical causes (material, formal, efficient, and final), and the God 'factor' at play in every natural happening, that is, the relation between God as primary cause and natural causes as secondary (created) causes. These doctrines are the set of tools in what I like to call Aquinas' metaphysical toolbox, tools which he employed when he discussed some particular theological doctrines, and those which Thomists today can also source for their work.

Following this, I will discuss different topics from the natural sciences with which Thomists have engaged throughout the twentieth and twenty-first centuries. Starting with quantum mechanics, I will show how it opened the path for the reintroduction of formal causes, reinterpreting the doctrine of degrees of being, and rethinking how divine providence can be understood to be active through the indeterminate processes of nature. I will, then, delve into cosmology, starting with some early encounters, followed by how Thomists interpreted Big Bang cosmology and the multiverse, and engagements with recent developments in astrobiology. Evolutionary biology will be the subject of the following section, being perhaps the topic that awoke more disagreement among Thomists, ranging from a complete dismissal up to a metaphysical acceptance of the evolutive origin of species. I will present this development within Thomism chronologically, with a final part devoted to the contemporary challenges arising from the problem of evil and original sin. Finally, I will bring forth several other topics in which Thomists currently work engaging their received Thomistic wisdom with the contemporary natural sciences: the

---

[13] Tanzella-Nitti 2023 offers a review of some dealings of late Thomism with the natural sciences.

cognitive sciences, human enhancement, the possibility of miracles, and the origin of life, ecology, and embryology.

2 Some Preliminary Definitions

2.1 Science-engaged Thomism

The next few pages will be devoted to discussing the benefits and merits of a different strategy within Thomism, suggesting how Thomists could re-engage with contemporary science. I do not claim that this strategy has not been followed before within this school or that it is not currently being pursued; as I hope to show in the coming pages, there are many scholars who offer inspiring engagements of science and Thomism, both in philosophy of nature and in theology. Still, identifying this methodology will also benefit this theological school in terms of its dialogue with others.

Thomas Aquinas assumed a similar strategy when facing some questions that the theology of his time posed when they related to the knowledge of the natural world. As a thirteenth-century scholar, Aquinas embraced the most up-to-date philosophical and theological problems of his time, addressing the most pressing and determining problems he and his contemporaries faced. While sourcing much of his thought from Augustine and the wisdom of the Fathers, Aquinas also incorporated the ill-reputed Aristotelian philosophy that had recently arrived from Muslim sources. This attitude meant he had, for some, the image of a heterodox thinker rather than that of the orthodox scholar we often assume. He appropriated the most modern of ideas concerning nature and the natural world and, acknowledging their 'modernity', he addressed theological problems of his present and past. In a way, Aquinas was engaging theology with the best knowledge of the natural world for attempting solutions for discrete theological problems. It is true that his search was for philosophical and theological wisdom and in this his pursuit was different from contemporary theology; but, in this search, he was solving discrete theological questions: one only needs to look at the way in which his *Summa Theologiae* or his commentary on Peter Lombard's *Sentences* is structured into questions and articles.

This strategy for approaching theological matters, resourcing to issues of nature when needed, could be compared to what John Perry and Joanna Leidenhag have recently described as science-engaged theology.[14] Perry and Leidenhag suggest that this approach should, instead of seeking grand comparisons between the sciences and the religions, 'study narrowly-focused theological questions that are already entangled with scientific theories and

---

[14] See Perry and Leidenhag 2023.

findings'.[15] For them, science-engaged theology should ask empirical questions to contemporary science, which is conceived, thus, as a material source for theological inquiry. To a certain extent, this is what Aquinas did when trying to solve different theological questions sourcing for that purpose the best knowledge of the natural world he had at hand, namely, the Aristotelian philosophy of nature. Consider, for instance, his discussions on the Eucharist and his use of the Aristotelian notions of substance and accidents, or his commentary on the *Hexameron* with the recurring illustrations of Aristotelian cosmology and geography, and the like,[16] which can be thought of as resembling this science-engaged theology of which Perry and Leidenhag speak.

When considering the question about the location of the Garden of Eden,[17] for instance, Aquinas sources the best geographical knowledge he had at hand. To the objection that men had already *diligentissime* (that is, very thoroughly) explored the whole of the habitable world and that no one had mentioned the Garden at all, Aquinas suggests that Eden is shut off from us by some natural impediment that cannot be crossed: Eden would be on the other side of either the impassable mountains (probably to the East, i.e., the Hindu-Kush range or even the Himalayas, which Alexander the Great did not manage to pass), or the great sea (probably to the West, the Atlantic Ocean, which was only crossed more than two centuries after), or the torrid central section of the globe (which for Aristotle was impenetrable). Eden was, hence, impossible to access, but was located on Earth.

Another rather interesting example of a theological puzzle comes from the consideration of the Incarnation of the Second Person of the Trinity. His Aristotelian approach to the question whether the flesh of Christ was conceived of the Virgin's purest blood (*ex purissimis sanguinibus virginis*) served not only as to provide an answer but also helped to shape the very question itself. The term *purissimis* was usually understood in the spiritual sense of Mary being the purest of creatures. Aquinas' reply shows how Aristotle's reproductive biology reconfigured the question, assuming the term *purissimis sanguinibus* biologically as well as spiritually, that is, as the purest blood out of which the flesh of a new human being was made. When explaining human reproduction, Aristotle teaches that the male and female seeds are formed as the final heightening of the blood's potential for form. Assuming the divine intervention (due to the lack of the male seed), Aquinas explains that the female principle of generation was 'the woman's blood brought to a more perfect stage of secretion by the mother's generative power'.[18] By affirming that Mary provided the blood in the most

---

[15] See Perry and Leidenhag 2021, 247.
[16] For other examples not referenced here, see Beltrán 2009, and Silva and Recio 2023.
[17] *S.Th.* I, 102, 1, *ad* 3.   [18] *S.Th.* III, 31, 5.

perfect stage, Aquinas reinterprets the very question as a reference both to Mary's holiness and virginity and also to the fact that the blood on which God acted was, biologically speaking, at its highest perfection. Ultimately, Aristotle's biological teachings helped Aquinas to understand better one of Christianity's core beliefs, while at the same time reconfiguring a question which would not have been set up in that way had he not been working within such a biological framework.

What matters in these examples is not the actual answer, but the way for approaching a discrete theological question. On the first one, Aquinas had previously followed the opinion of the Fathers and explained that the Garden was somewhere in the East. Still, he opens up the theological game in the replies to the objections. The theological question regarding the *earthly place* of Eden required the use of empirical data (understood in the broadest possible sense) that was brought about by philosophers, explorers, and historians. Relying on the testimony of other authorities on the natural world of the time, Aquinas considers the data and finds that Eden *could* be located elsewhere, beyond the infrangible sea, mountains, or desert. On the second example, Aquinas accepts the usual interpretation of *purissimis* as referring to a spiritual sense, but again moves the theological boundaries beyond the traditional path and making use of Aristotelian reproductive biology offers a new twist to a key theological matter. Thus, Aquinas' appeal to the knowledge of the natural world offered by medieval natural philosophy shows the importance that he gave to this kind of knowledge for his theological enterprise. This strategy bares quite a resemblance to today's science-engaged theology.

Some early twentieth-century Thomism engagements with the natural sciences offer some contrasts with this strategy. I have referred to the revival of Thomism after the impulse of Pope Leo XIII, who had three goals in mind, the third of which is of every importance to this narrative. His call was to restore the wisdom of St. Thomas 'for the defence and beauty of the Catholic faith, for the good of society, and *for the advantage of all the sciences*'.[19] That is, the sciences would gain much from their interaction with the philosophical and theological thought of Thomas Aquinas. This papal call was, at least at times, understood in the sense that Thomists should produce something like Thomism-engaged science. Rather than making use of contemporary science to delve deeper into the mystery of creation and the divine, some Thomism mapped science into Thomist jargon, so to speak.

I do not want to claim that this is a completely unfortunate strategy to engage with the sciences. Thomism-engaged science could certainly have

---

[19] Pope Leo XIII 1879, §31 (my emphasis).

something of value to offer to the natural sciences and the philosophy of science. In fact, Werner Heisenberg, for instance, somehow claimed for this when in his 1955–1956 Gifford Lectures on *Physics and Philosophy*, rejecting the Cartesian philosophy of pure actuality, he suggested adopting the two Aristotelian fundamental notions of act and potency. From Thomistic camps, some decades earlier – the very same year when Heisenberg published his uncertainty principle – Petrus Hoenen, SJ (1880–1961), who held a doctorate in physics, claimed that the new physics would be 'be Aristotelean-Thomistic or it will not be'.[20] Similarly, by the end of the twentieth century, Dutch philosopher Leo Elders (1926–2019) claimed that, in sight of the new atomic theory, 'we should continue holding the doctrine of the essential nature of things according to which the underlying substance of material things is the bearer of their properties and functions'.[21]

My suggestion, thus, is for a methodological turn in Thomist engagements with the natural sciences, a turn from assuming that Aquinas' thought can be construed as a closed philosophical or theological system that solves all conundrums and tensions between science and faith, and to construct this science-engaged Thomism, a strategy that closely follows Aquinas' own example. Certainly, this new methodology does not neglect the ample Thomistic tradition in philosophy and theology, but rather hopes to reinvigorate it by approaching theological questions with a set of metaphysical and scientific tools that, together, are helpful to solve these questions.

Peter Harrison has reflected on the new science-engaged theology, suggesting three challenges that it sets to avoid: 'a pattern of subservience in which science always trumps theology; an anti-science agenda that either rejects the legitimacy of science or denies that it has anything useful to offer theologians; an assertion of the total independence of science and theology that disavows any significant points of contact'.[22] Science-engaged Thomism could certainly avoid these pitfalls as well, even if some past Thomism has failed to do so. In fact, Thomism is usually confronted with the objection that, by posing itself at a different level of analysis (be it in the metaphysics of being or the hylomorphic philosophy of nature), it simply distances itself from any scientific discourse. Science-engaged Thomism wants to approach the study of nature and the divine hand-in-hand with the natural sciences, for the simple reason that one knows God from His effects. This approach could, as Harrison suggests, 'afford us new opportunities to reimagine aspects of a Christian tradition that had been lost as a consequence of habits of mind that arise out of modern concepts and ideas'.[23] In fact, the search for a Thomistic 'system',

---

[20] As quoted in Flipse 2008, 1149. [21] Elders 1997. [22] Harrison 2021, 476.
[23] Harrison 2021, 478.

the great project of early twentieth-century Neo-Thomism, could be seen as one of those not so beneficial habits of mind arising out of modernity.

This Thomistic approach would consider theological questions as Aquinas did seeking for relevant connections to the different sciences for solving some of those issues. Following on Harrison's suggestions, rather than defending itself against the findings of science, science-engaged Thomism would, being true to Aquinas' spirit, make use of the tools and resources that the sciences have on offer to progress in its solutions to new and pressing philosophical and theological questions.[24] As I mentioned at the outset of this section, I do not want to claim this is new to Thomism, but that it is good to recognise it as a way of practicing philosophy and theology within it. As Simon Kopf expressed it, science-engaged Thomism 'would seem to have a claim on being a form of Thomism, although it may not be a new form of Thomism ... What is perhaps new is the explicit emphasis on the importance of engaging the sciences'.[25]

Science-engaged Thomism, thus, emphasises the openness that Aquinas had towards being informed in his theological work by the best knowledge of the natural world. The levels of this engagement will vary and, ultimately, depend on the issue at stake. In fact, Aquinas' examples open the path to a large array of possibilities. Thus, there will be theological problems that are scientifically informed, others that would be scientifically backed, while others would simply engage in a comparative dialogue for mutual enrichment. Furthermore, Aquinas' also exemplifies the possibility of engaging with philosophical reflections about this very knowledge of the natural world. In a way, science-engaged Thomism also confirms John Brooke's teachings about the complex relations between science and religion in history, assuming that there is a diversity of possible interactions at many different levels between the natural sciences and Thomist philosophy and theology.[26]

Certainly, the Thomist could do philosophy or theology in a different way. One could simply be addressing philosophical or theological questions that have no intersection with the natural sciences, and in that case, one would need not engage with them. Or one could engage with other sciences besides the natural sciences. Kopf expresses it wonderfully: 'Thomism should *also* be science-engaged, in appropriate cases – just as Thomism should, for instance, be at times Scripture-engaged, Tradition-engaged, or philosophy-engaged'.[27] What I am suggesting is, simply, that the thought of Thomas Aquinas has the potential of engaging with the natural sciences in imaginative ways as Thomas Aquinas did in his time.

---

[24] Science-engaged Thomism, thus, is not an apologetic enterprise.   [25] Kopf 2024, 8–9.
[26] See Silva and Recio 2023. Brooke 1991.   [27] Kopf 2024, 7.

If my claim that (1) science-engaged Thomism is sound, that (2) it would rightfully follow the example set by Aquinas on how to address certain theological questions, and (3) that such an enterprise is viable, then there must be certain examples to describe it. In fact, I find it in the works of many contemporary Thomists around the globe, and many of the topics these scholars address, as it would be expected, find their genesis in the thought of Aquinas himself. Perry and Leidenhag have identified one of Alvin Plantinga's ideas as the leading motto for science-engaged theology. They refer to Alvin Plantinga when he claimed that 'the world, as God created it, is full of contingencies. Therefore, we do not merely think about it in our armchairs, trying to infer from first principles how many teeth there are in a horse's mouth; instead, we take a look'.[28] The Italian philosopher and Jesuit priest Filippo Selvaggi (1913–1995) has expressed this same idea in the following terms in relation to Thomism, saying that it, 'in fact, is not a purely rational and necessary philosophy, in the Platonic, Cartesian or Hegelian sense ... but a philosophy that is essentially empirical and rational at the same time, open therefore, to every experience, while firmly maintaining the inalienable absolute values of reason'.[29] This is nothing but a call for Thomists to engage with the sciences in order to understand the world and God better and more profoundly.

2.2 The Thomist's Metaphysical Toolbox

Thomas Aquinas set up a metaphysical toolbox for us. This toolbox is mostly composed by the most general notions of hylomorphism, in addition to final and efficient causation, plus his ideas on the relation between primary and secondary causes, that is, divine and created causes, to account for how God acts providentially in the universe. Even if one is used to these notions, it might be useful to revisit them quickly.

The four causes with which Aquinas explained the works of the natural world are well known: material, formal, efficient, and final. For Aquinas, matter is that which remains when a thing changes into another, which means two things: (1) that it is 'that from which a thing is made',[30] and (2) that it is not one thing or another, but rather that it is in potency to contraries. The first of these should be understood not in the sense that matter is something inside the thing but, rather, as something inherent to the very thing of which it is the matter. Upon it, thus, the thing depends for its being: were matter not there, the thing would cease to

---

[28] Perry and Leidenhag 2021, 248.   [29] Selvaggi 1962, 148.   [30] *In V Met.* l. 2.

be.³¹ For material beings, not having matter means non-existing. Now, given that matter is potency for receiving forms, it receives the form and participates its own material being to the form, that is, because of the materiality of the material cause, the thing is material. The second idea refers to matter's potential character. The material cause is a purely potential principle with the capacity for acquiring and having one or another form, but it cannot be devoid of any form, because it will simply not be. Hence, it is the root of being capable of becoming something different from what a thing is.

Matter requires a second principle to actualise its potentiality and make it be something, that is, the form. The form is that which makes a thing be and be what it is actualising matter. As with matter, forms are not 'inside' things. On the contrary, it is the second intrinsic co-principle by which natural things are and are what they are. Thus, both form and matter bring into existence the individual thing. Natural things, then, depend upon their form: were the form not causing them to be what they are they would simply not be.³² A thing, thus, is this kind of thing, and not another, through its own form, because the form brings to actuality the potentiality of matter. Still, things can change and will most probably do so, which means that not all the potentiality of matter is actualised; hence, things are a mixture of potentiality or indetermination and actuality or determination.

Now, a thing receives from its form all of what it is, including the way in which it acts and operates. Thus, 'each thing acts according to its form, which is the principle of action'.³³ In other words, forms provide things with their powers to act. Behaviours, actions, and reactions are natural for any given thing, precisely to the extent that they proceed from within it, and thus from its matter and form as its basic constituents.

Now, given that matter's potentiality cannot be actualised on its own without a cause that actualises it,³⁴ it is necessary that there be an efficient cause to produce this passage from potency to the actual receiving of a new form. To cause as an efficient cause, thus, is to make something go, in any respect, from potency to act. Every efficient cause acts, however, due to its possessing this or that form, and so it does something that bears some resemblance or similarity to that form.³⁵ Sometimes it is the same form, when fire produces fire, or a horse another horse, and sometimes it is a different form, as when a man builds a house.³⁶ The latter type is possible because the power of the efficient cause exceeds the potentiality of the matter receiving the action.

---

³¹ *De Pot.*, q. 5, a. 1, co.   ³² *De Pot.*, q. 5, a. 1, co.   ³³ *In De Causis*, l. 8.
³⁴ *In III De An.*, l. 9.   ³⁵ *De Pot.*, q. 7, a. 5, co.   ³⁶ *De Malo*, q. 1, a. 3, co.

Still, efficient causes could fail and become deficient causes not causing what they were ordered to cause according to their forms. This shows that efficient causes act towards something, tend to produce certain effects. This is why Aquinas speaks of final causes. A final cause, then, is the that for which the efficient cause causes; it is as a natural tendency in things to act in this or that manner.[37] For Aquinas, were there no final causes, things would not do anything, since they would have no natural inclination to behave in this or that way. Final causes trigger actions, and, in that respect, they are causal, they are purposeful natural behaviours that can be described as acts directed towards a goal or an end. They originate in the formal cause of things, since these are the principle of action in natural things.

As I said, Aquinas acknowledged that natural things may or may not accomplish the effect to which their nature tends.[38] Since natural things are contingent in their being, and given that action follows being, they can fail in their natural actions. To account for this possibility, Aquinas distinguishes between events that happen almost always (*ut in pluribus*) and those that happen rarely but do happen sometimes (*ut in paucioribus*). Aquinas explains the latter in reference to the intrinsic causes of things, that is, the material and the formal cause, suggesting that these events have their ultimate root in the material cause of natural things.

The role of the material cause is threefold: (1) in reference to the efficient cause in itself; (2) as the matter on which the efficient cause acts; (3) in reference to the encounter of many efficient causes. In the first one, the material cause, as principle of pure passive capacity of being, becomes the origin of the defectiveness in the action of the natural efficient cause, thus making it weak, so to speak, and causing the possibility of not causing what the efficient cause was meant to cause. In the second one, the material cause of the thing that receives the action, once again as principle of potentiality, could allow for some indeterminacy in the way that the effect is produced. So, even if the efficient cause causes what is expected, it is still possible that the effect would not be produced. The third one refers to the conjunction of a series of efficient causes, in which the plurality of causes is, in itself, indefinite, that is, accidental, since it does not have any natural determinate efficient cause. Basically, the conjunction does not cause a chanceful event; it is the very effect of chance. So, Aquinas holds that, given the material principle in things, there always exists the possibility for them to fail in their actions. For material things, then, given their intrinsic hylomorphic, will always behave with a certain degree of indeterminism and contingency, the source of which is the material co-principle.

---

[37] *In V Met.*, l. 2. [38] *SCG* III, c. 64.

The key to many questions relating the natural sciences and Thomistic theology relies on the solution Aquinas suggests to the problem of divine providential action, which is embedded in his account of God as pure act and as the creative source of all being. Given the contingent existence of natural things, Aquinas affirms the existence of a being that possesses existence by its own nature, that is, a being the existence of which is not caused, and thus can cause the existence of all other beings. Now, Aquinas understands this being to be God. And because existence is pure act, God is pure act, meaning that God lacks any kind of passive potency. Therefore, since in things there is a distinction between their essence and their existence, God is not a 'thing', meaning that God does not belong to the natural order of things, that is, God transcends things.[39] This transcendence is usually explained by way of participation:[40] the being that possesses existence by its own essence can participate it to other beings. Thus, natural things receive their being by way of participation.

This giving of being by way of participation is what Aquinas understands *creatio ex nihilo* to be. This notion includes the very gift of existence to created things, as well as the kind of thing and, thus, the way things act. That is, God communicates or participates not only His being to natural things, but in doing so, God also communicates His power to creatures. Thus, since natural things act according to the power that God gives them, Aquinas will argue that God acts in nature by participating his power to natural things. This is the metaphysical reason for affirming that the creature depends for its existence on the creator, whereas the creator does not depend at all on the creature.[41]

Aquinas refers to the idea of creation to offer a first glance at his distinction between primary and secondary causation. Causation of being belongs to the first universal cause, whereas causation of all that is in addition to being belongs to secondary causes that act by information, that is, by giving the form to the effect. God is the primary cause of things because God causes the very existence of all created things, without which things would simply not be.[42] Thus, the secondary cause cannot do anything if it is not by way of the primary cause causing it to be.[43] So, even if the secondary cause is the real cause of its effect, the primary cause is primarily the cause of the effect of the secondary cause. Thus, since the secondary cause does not cause except by participating in the power of the primary cause, the effect does not proceed from the power of the secondary cause except because of the participated power of the primary cause.

---

[39] See *S.Th.* I, q. 12, a. 2. [40] *In De Causis*, l. 4. [41] *De Pot.*, q. 3, a. 3, co.
[42] *In De Causis*, l. 3. And *In De Causis*, l. 18. [43] *In De Causis*, l. 9.

In a great understatement – perhaps the greatest – Aquinas suggests that 'it seems difficult for some to understand how natural effects are attributed to God and to a natural cause',[44] which is the basis for understanding Aquinas' own doctrine of providence. He offers, thus, four ways in which God can be said to be acting in nature, each of which portrays God to be more present and intimate in the creature than the previous.

First, something is said to cause the action of another by giving the power to act, which is what happens in creation. As I said, when God creates, God gives both the being something and the powers that come with that being.[45] Second, God may also be said to cause the action of creatures by upholding that created power in existence. As a remedy that preserves sight is said to make a man see, any action that stops after the influence of a certain cause ceases is attributed to that efficient cause.[46] Similarly, were the divine preservation of created powers in existence to cease, all created actions would disappear. I have previously called these two the 'foundational moments' of God acting in creation. I have used the term 'dynamic moments' for the remaining two.

The final two ways depend on Aquinas' teachings on instrumental causes. For Aquinas, a thing is the cause of another's action when the first moves the second to act, which is usually called the application of the causal power of an instrument to action. For example, when someone uses the cutting power of a knife by applying its sharpness to cutting a loaf of bread, or when someone uses a pen to write a letter to a friend. In this kind of action, the effect of the instrument can be considered in a twofold manner: first, as an effect that pertains to the instrument according to its nature; and second as an effect that pertains to it insofar as it is moved by the primary cause and that transcends the nature of the instrument.

In Aquinas' model of divine causation, each of these manners refers to each of the two dynamic moments. The first of these two ways of causing refers to the first manner of considering the effect of an instrumental cause. God moves every created cause to act according to its own nature and powers to achieve its proper effect. The second way of causing the action of the instrument refers to the second manner of understanding the effect of an instrumental cause, that is, as causing something that goes beyond the power of created causes.

Thus, for Aquinas, God is at work in every operation of every creature as the initial cause of its power to act, as the preserver of that power (the foundational moments), as applying it to action, and inasmuch as creatures reach effects that go beyond their powers (the dynamic moments). Thus, the same effect is

---

[44] *SCG* III, c. 70. [45] *SCG* III, c. 67. [46] *SCG* III, c. 67.

attributed to a creature and to God, not as if part of the effect were caused by God and part by the creature: each cause the whole effect, yet in different ways, as the whole of the one same effect is attributed to the instrument and to the principal cause.

Thus, God gives natural things the power to perform their operations according to their own forms, and in doing so God acts as first cause requiring, in a way, the power of the secondary cause, and so preserving the order of things. For Aquinas, this does not imply that God does not have the sufficient power to cause what is done through creatures. Instead, God acts through creatures because of the immensity of His goodness, participating His power to creatures, thus providing them with the dignity of being real causes.

Aquinas metaphysical analysis of God's nature and power leads to see God as the continuous giver of being and powers. This creative action implies the utter dependence of creatures upon God, God being profoundly immanent to creation. That is, God has a transcendent-immanent character towards creation: God is radically distinct from creation and God is profoundly present and active within it. God's influence extends to all things as God is most intimately present in each thing. Aquinas' doctrine of creation, thus, offers an account of how and why things are and why they act as they do. His account emphasises that as creatures participate in God's being to exist, they also participate in God's power to act.

Therefore, God can be thought of as continuously active within the universe acting in every action of creatures. Still, the first cause does not interfere with the causality of a secondary cause but is rather the source of that causality. Now, even if God's activity is present in all things, it is not merely generic. Instead, it is fundamentally a particular activity through each secondary cause. Finally, in this continuous action, God could also bring about effects beyond the nature of creatures.

3 Quantum Mechanics

Perhaps the most surprising of all scientific advances of the twentieth century was the development of quantum theory. It comprises a set of principles that describe physical reality and its behaviour at the atomic and sub-atomic levels. It is, no doubt, among the most successful scientific theories but also one of the most puzzling ones. The success includes explaining phenomena such as the stability of atoms, the nature of chemical bonds, the strengths and colours of materials, ferromagnetism, and the colours of hot bodies in equilibrium with their hot surroundings. These phenomena are now well understood on the basis of the mathematical formalism of quantum mechanics. This mathematical formalism, however, appears to bring about features of reality that appeared to be most implausible, like the wave-particle duality, the superposition principle, or the entanglement property of pairs of particles. Still, perhaps the most striking of all phenomena is the indeterministic character that the new physics discovers in the quantum world. Heisenberg's uncertainty principle, first proposed in February of 1927,[47] affirms that it is conceptually impossible to determine simultaneously the position and the momentum (or any other pair of conjugate quantities) of one single particle. According to this principle, since it is impossible to know the initial state of a system absolutely, it will also be impossible to determine the future of that system. The only possible knowledge of that future will be a probabilistic or statistical knowledge. Now, following the so-called Copenhagen orthodox interpretation of quantum mechanics, this probabilistic character of the theory has been taken to point towards a fundamental ontological indeterminism found in the quantum realm. Thus, this orthodox interpretation affirms that the probability statements made by quantum mechanics are irreducible in the sense that they do not exclusively reflect our limited knowledge of the system. Instead, quantum systems are fundamentally indeterministic.

As I mentioned earlier in this Element, Heisenberg reads this ontological indeterminism through the lens of the Aristotelian notions of act and potency: 'One might perhaps call it an objective tendency or possibility, a *potentia* in the sense of Aristotelian philosophy. In fact, I believe that the language actually used by physicists when they speak about atomic events produces in their minds similar notions as the concept *potentia*.'[48] In contrast to what he saw happening in classical physics, Heisenberg describes a new ontology for quantum physics,[49] in which besides the actual, the potential is also real, that is, what is in potency is real. For Heisenberg, quantum reality is indeterminate, open to different actualisations. The transition from the 'possible' to the 'actual', Heisenberg adds, takes place during the act of observation or measurement. That is, as soon as the interaction of the object with the measuring device, and thereby with the rest of the world, occurs, one of the possibilities in the system becomes actual.[50] This new ontology inspired new insights in Thomist perspectives about God and God's creation. There are at least two, one of which refers to the very being of God in relation to creation, while the second one refers to God's providential action in the natural world. Before these, however, some twentieth-century, as well as contemporary, Thomists have seen in this new

---

[47] Heisenberg 1927.   [48] Heisenberg 1958, 180–181.   [49] Heisenberg 1958, 185.
[50] Heisenberg 1958, 54.

ontology a rejection of a strong mechanical atomism that has given place to a new discourse about forms in the natural world.

3.1 Quantum Mechanics and the Re-Introduction of Forms

As soon as quantum theory started to move beyond the circles of pure physics, several Thomist scholars engaged with it in their philosophies of nature. To name but a few, one may refer to the works of mid twentieth-century Jesuits Petrus Hoenen and Filippo Selvaggi or more recent developments in the works of the philosophers Robert Koons and William M. R. Simpson (both of whom might rather identify themselves as Neo-Aristotelians, though much of the Thomist tradition can be found in their ideas) as well as Edward Feser.

Perhaps the very first problem to solve was whether the new science of the twentieth century favoured the basic Aristotelian notion of substance, as that which subsists by itself, which led to the reintroduction of the notion of form, after its demise by the mechanistic philosophy behind the rise of modern science. Filippo Selvaggi found in de Broglie's interpretation of the wave-particle duality a basis on which to reconstruct Aristotelian substances. For Selvaggi, de Broglie 'recognises as equally primary and objective both the undulatory and corpuscular aspects and try to form some image that allows this reconciliation'.[51] As such, 'the elements that compose mixtures [nuclei, atoms, molecules] are not mechanical corpuscles, exactly localised, intrinsically immutable, which follow a determinate and continuous path in their local motion, like some rigid and minimally dimensioned ball, but are like diffuse and fluctuating waves, penetrating each other, intrinsically mutable, like more or less concentrated energy'.[52]

In fact, faced with the fact that much in quantum mechanics is not massive, that is, it does not possess mass (such as fields, waves, and even the quantum vacuum), Selvaggi suggests expanding the notion of material substance to these also by applying Aquinas' definition of material substance. One finds that Aquinas has affirmed that a body 'insofar as it is in the genera of substance, is said to have such a nature that three dimensions can be designed in it'.[53] So, Selvaggi suggests that, in the most general sense, a material substance is mobile and extended, thus implying that not only bodies, in the sense of classical physics, but also fields, waves, empty space, in short all the concepts used by quantum physics, are included in this notion.[54]

Now, given several features that befall onto these substances, Selvaggi finds that the best explanation for them is hylomorphism. For instance, Selvaggi

---

[51] Selvaggi 1959, 249. [52] Selvaggi 1959, 272. [53] *De Ente*, ch. 1.
[54] Selvaggi 1962, 148.

mentions, 'the virtual presence of electrons and positrons in atomic nuclei, composed of only protons and neutrons, yet capable of emitting electrons and positrons in radioactive transformations; the spontaneous or induced transformation of elementary particles into other specifically different elementary particles, protons, neutrons, mesons, hyperons, etc.; the so-called creation and annihilation of pairs of antithetical particles (electrons and positrons, protons and antiprotons, etc.) with absorption or emission of a quantum of light',[55] and many other phenomena. For him, such events cannot be fully explained by mechanistic atomism, given that these substances cannot be thought of as mere aggregates and even their causal powers cannot be the result of the aggregation of their parts.[56] Thus, Selvaggi claims that 'hylomorphic theory, is recognised as indispensable in modern physics, in nuclear physics and in elementary particle physics ... [which] allows us to maintain the causal explanatory value of science, not reducing it to a pure phenomenal description'.[57]

This realist take on scientific knowledge, and in particular of the realism of quantum physics, moved Selvaggi to offer a reinterpretation of the Catholic dogma of transubstantiation in the sacrament of the Eucharist.[58] Even if somewhat heterodox in his presentation, which did certainly spark some reactions and criticisms against it,[59] Selvaggi's proposal portrays the audacity of some twentieth-century Thomists in engaging with science, audacity that, as I showed earlier, Thomas Aquinas had in his time. The dogma, as defined by the Council of Trent in the sixteenth century, states that the whole of the substance of bread and the whole of the substance of wine turn in to the whole of the substance of the body and blood of Christ. Selvaggi acknowledges that for Aquinas, who followed the knowledge of his time, bread was a natural kind, but suggests that contemporary science does not allow us to hold on to that view. So, not being bread a natural kind, bread cannot be said to be a substance on its own, like living beings are. Thus, what really counts as bread is nothing more than its atomic and molecular constituents. However, Selvaggi asserts that the unity (i.e., the being one substance) of the bread and the wine is not at all necessary for the Eucharistic dogma. At this point of the argument the Italian Jesuit expresses the importance for the theologian to engage with the natural sciences: 'although it is not essential to the dogma and although it is not a question that can be

---

[55] Selvaggi 1962, 252–253.   [56] Selvaggi 1962, 269.   [57] Selvaggi 1962, 252–253.
[58] Selvaggi 1949, 7–45.
[59] The debate surrounding Selvaggi's Eucharistic proposal took place mostly during the 1950s and the early 1960s. Just to name a few papers, one can refer to Colombo 1955, 1956, 1960; Selvaggi 1956, 1957; Masi 1955, 1957. The debate has even attracted the attention of later English-speaking theologians: Clark 1951; Vollert 1961; Cipolla 1974.

solved with theological reasons, it may be of interest to the theologian to know what the physicist and the natural philosopher conclude on the matter'.[60]

Selvaggi, thus, affirms that

> modern science, in conclusion, no longer permits us to speak, as St. Thomas did, of a substantial form of bread [or wine], which informs and gives unity to an entire mass or even to a fragment of it ... The form of bread as such is an accidental form in the sense of scholastic philosophy ... ; that is, the form of bread [or wine] is that determined mixture of substances, obtained in that determined way.[61]

Bread and wine, for Selvaggi, are what is known in Aristotelian natural philosophy as aggregates, lacking internal unity, and thus not being properly speaking a substance on their own. Hence, what is meant in transubstantiation when the Council states that all the substance of the bread and wine is converted into Christ's body and blood, is that 'the protons, neutrons and electrons in act, which belong to the mass of the consecrated matter, the atoms, the molecules, the ions, the molecular complexes, the microcrystals, in short the whole set of substances that constitute the bread and wine, cease to be and are converted into the body and blood of Christ', while all the accidents pertaining to those substances remain, such as the 'the extension, the mass, the electric charges, with all the energies, potential and actual, magnetic, electric, kinetic, that derive from them, and therefore all the optical, acoustic, thermodynamic, electromagnetic effects, that those forces can produce'.[62] Given this permanence of the accidents after consecration, our senses and even our instruments will experience bread and wine, and they will not be mistaken in that experience. Still, Selvaggi continues, if with our intelligence following the results of the experiments, we were to conclude that there is bread or wine, we

> would fall into error, an error that is not detectable by the means of physics, nor by the reasonings of the intellect, but only by the light of faith. In this sense the Eucharistic dogma is completely outside the domain of physics and completely escapes scientific control and criticism; but in this same sense it also escapes the dominion and control of philosophy and human reason in general.[63]

As I mentioned earlier, Selvaggi's proposal awoke a full array of criticism and a heated debate. Still, his theological attitude towards the natural science as a Thomist could be thought of as beacon of how even Thomas Aquinas approached the knowledge of the natural world in the thirteenth century. A theology that is open to what the science of the time is to say about the

---

[60] Selvaggi 1949, 36.   [61] Selvaggi 1949, 42.   [62] Selvaggi 1949, 43.
[63] Selvaggi 1949, 44.

natural world is a science-engaged theology, and as such, Selvaggi becomes an example of a science-engaged Thomist theologian.

Resuming my considerations about the reintroduction of formal causes in the quantum world, British contemporary philosopher William Simpson seems to agree with Selvaggi, at least partially, with the realist perspective stated earlier. Simpson suggests the notion of hylomorphic pluralism, which 'affirms the existence of a variety of substances in nature which are metaphysically prior to their physical parts',[64] thus offering an alternative to microphysical reductionism, what Selvaggi would call mechanistic philosophy, and with which Peter Hoenen would also agree.[65] For Simpson's hylomorphic pluralism, entities (or substances) are metaphysically composed of matter and substantial form, with the causal powers of that entity being grounded in its substantial form. Thus, the parts of the substance are not themselves substances. Rather, the substantial form is the formal cause of the unity of the substance by determining the powers of its parts. Robert Koons explains this idea in reference to quantum physics stating that 'individual particles (and finite ensembles of particles, like atoms and molecules) seem to lose their individual identity . . . For the quantum hylomorphist, when particles participate in a substance, the fundamental physical attributes are possessed at the level of the substance as a whole, and only derivatively and dependently by the individual molecules'.[66]

Once again in agreement with Selvaggi's perspective, Simpson suggests that hylomorphic pluralism 'does not conceive of physical substances as existing in a state of causal isolation, but allows substances to interact with one another through the exercise of their causal powers'.[67] In fact, Selvaggi saw that 'arguments taken from modern physics certainly prove that physical reality is not composed of individual substances closed in themselves and immutable, but of substances that interact with each other . . . communicate with each other through the emission and absorption of quanta, which can probably be considered as substances and certainly establish some intimate exchange between interacting substances'.[68] Finally, Simpson, as Selvaggi, offers a realist account of quantum mechanics grounded in his hylomorphic pluralism: '[The] Hylomorphic Pluralist is committed to a realist approach to quantum mechanics: the wave function governed by the non-linear Schrödinger equation represents a real power of the substance to regulate its own parcel of matter, which is grounded in its substantial form.'[69]

Certainly, as Koons has recently expressed, 'no one can be forced by quantum phenomena to embrace hylomorphism'. But, he continues, 'unlike the other

---

[64] Simpson 2022, 52. [65] See Hoenen 1956, 451 and 468–474. [66] Koons 2022, 157.
[67] Simpson 2022, 53. [68] Selvaggi 1959, 245. [69] Simpson 2022, 54.

interpretations, hylomorphism does not require any ad hoc modifications or unverifiable additions, and it accords best with the actual practice of science. Practicing quantum scientists, like everyone else, are implicit Aristotelians'.[70] In a way, as Feser suggests, 'quantum mechanics actually points towards Aristotelianism', or, one may even say, Thomism.[71] Given that the theory describes a world full of potentiality until actualised, it can be seen as 'pointing towards' hylomorphism and the theory of actuality and potentiality, as I have shown earlier that Heisenberg suggested.

3.2 The New Quantum Ontology and the Degrees of Being

In a clear Neo-Platonic take of God's relation to the created universe, many Thomists of the twentieth century have attempted at a reincorporation of the metaphysical notion of the degrees of being as such.[72] The surfacing of this new ontology in quantum mechanics for which Heisenberg advocated allowed many to bring back to the fore the idea that there is a gradual metaphysical hierarchy of being, which can be described in terms of active and passive determinism and indeterminism.

For Aquinas, pure act and pure potency are the two extremes of a hierarchy that finds in God, the source of all being, and in pure prime matter those two opposites. In this hierarchy, act and potency are mixed in a higher or lower proportion according to each thing's relation to either pole. Thus, those closest to pure act would have a greater actuality and those closest to pure potency would have lesser actuality. As one descends in the degrees of being, the corresponding reduction in actuality correlates with an increase in potentiality, down to the forms of the elements, which are the closest to prime matter, pure potency. Greater or lesser actuality comes from the participated being. Hence, those things that are closer to prime matter would be those that would have lesser actuality and greater potentiality. The farther the thing is from pure actuality, that is, God, the greater its potentiality. With greater actuality, there is more determination in being, whereas with lesser actuality, there is a greater indetermination in being. That is, there is an active determination that is opposed to a passive indetermination, which finds its root in the remoteness from that being that is pure act, namely, God. Natural things, as they are farther from pure act, participate less in act: they are less determinate. Hence, they are more potential, and with this their passive indetermination increases. Now, considering this passive indeterminism found at the lower levels of reality,

---

[70] Koons 2022, 157. [71] Feser 2019, 310.
[72] See, for instance, de Koninck 1937, as well as Selvaggi 1964.

given the greater potentiality and lesser actuality that things possess at these levels, their effects will be uncertain.

This is precisely what can be seen experimentally at the level of quantum mechanics, which served Heisenberg to speak of a new ontology and served some Thomists to retrieve the doctrine of the degrees of being in Aquinas' thought (such as Filippo Selvaggi or the Belgian-Canadian philosopher Charles De Koninck). It is at this level in which what occurs can only be disclosed experientially, because the passive indetermination is the reason for a fundamental unpredictability in events.[73] It does not sound implausible to affirm that quantum mechanics is working with and describing natural things that are great in potency and low in act, possibly reaching those forms of natural things that are closest to what in the Aristotelian ontology has been called prime matter. This was Heisenberg's intuition when claiming that sub-atomic particles were in potency before being observed, and Feser expressed it quite straightforwardly: 'the most natural way to account for the mysteriousness of quantum phenomena is in terms of their proximity to the indeterminacy of prime matter'.[74] Evidently, they cannot be pure potency, as Heisenberg wanted, because they would be prime matter itself, which cannot exist without some form. Quantum physics, being open to experience, cannot deny the existence of a certain causal indeterminism, which, as Heisenberg suggested, is not reducible to the epistemological order, but is rooted in the ontological order of things, given primarily by the potentiality of matter.[75]

The real potentiality found at the quantum level, potentiality at such a great level that allows for experimentally detecting indeterminism in nature, called for a reconsideration of the doctrine of the degrees of being in Thomist metaphysics, and in understanding the relation that pure act, God, has with pure potentiality and indeterminism.

In fact, the postulation of a passive indeterminism referred to the postulation of an active indeterminism that comes from perfection in being, and that is represented paradigmatically, in Aquinas' thought, by the free will present in spiritual beings. In God's case, God's pure actuality represents an absolute determination, which is the root of His active indetermination that is essentially a perfection. God is absolutely free. This active indetermination is based on the plenitude of actuality, in as much as God's actuality represents an unlimited capacity for participating God's own perfection to other created beings.[76] Any participated active indetermination is founded in the very determination of God's being. As such, one finds active indetermination without free will in

---

[73] Selvaggi 1964, 153. [74] Feser 2019, 322. [75] Selvaggi 1964, 386–388.
[76] Selvaggi 1964, 151.

the created world. Plants and animals exhibit this active indetermination in their spontaneity, and in this their behaviour is also unpredictable. As long as the created beings participate in the actuality of the pure act, they also participate in its active indetermination, which is greatest in purely immaterial spirits (God and the angels) and becomes lesser in material beings as one descends in the metaphysical hierarchy of the degrees of being. There is, thus, a constant directly proportional relation between the degree of participation of the thing in God's being and its active and passive indetermination.[77]

3.3 Divine Providence and Indeterminism

In a similar way in which twentieth-century developments in quantum mechanics offered the opportunity for Thomists to reflect about the metaphysical roots of indeterminism in nature by referring to the doctrine of the degrees of being, this same scientific theory inspired a rediscovery of Aquinas' thought on providence and its relation to natural indeterminism. The question on providential divine action in the natural world in light of the new scientific developments of quantum mechanics gave rise to several different alternative answers, ranging from quantum divine action (in which God would actualise a possible outcome of a quantum event)[78] to divine action through chaotic dynamical systems (in which God would input active information that would govern the behaviour of such systems).[79]

Confronted with this scenario, Thomists approached the debate arguing that God could not be regarded as a secondary cause, or, in Thomist jargon, as a cause among causes, as these proposals tended to imply. In addition, many argued that God acted always as the creator and sustainer of creation in existence, and hence was not a secondary cause. This argument, present in the works of numerous scholars such as William Stoeger,[80] was challenged as an untenable position, since it rendered God either the cause of everything or the cause of nothing, leaving the question about the relation between divine and natural action unsolved (or solved in an unsatisfactory way, simply negating one of the relata).[81] These objections pushed Thomists to revise their own position and a new fuller version of the relation between primary and secondary causation was proposed. This new version reaffirmed divine creation and sustainment in existence, but dug out two further moments of divine action, namely, those of

---

[77] de Koninck 1937, 237. [78] See Russell 2006. [79] See Polkinghorne 2000.
[80] Stoeger 1995, 253.
[81] See, for instance, the objection presented by Clayton 2004 or Polkinghorne 1995. See also a reply to them in Silva 2013. New objections were raised in Sollereder 2015 and Kittle 2022, with Lazzari (2025) offering a new reply to these.

applying the secondary cause to act, understood in terms of instrumental causation, as described earlier.

In a non-trivial sense, the indeterminism found in quantum mechanics allowed Thomists to rediscover a fuller metaphysical explanation of providential divine action, with which to account for God's involvement in the world, even through indeterminate events at different levels of the natural world. For Aquinas, natural secondary causes at all levels of reality are somewhat contingent in their activity and in their causal capacities, being, thus, indeterminate to their effects, as I explained earlier. Those causes that are most indeterminate can, then, be the most deficient causes. This deficient causation implies the causing of a lack of *being* in their effects. God, then, is thought to allow this type of events, because God, acting as the primary cause, can bring about new instances of being out of them according to the divine intention. As the first cause of all actions of created beings, God is the cause of all there is of being caused by the secondary cause in the effect, as I showed above. When indeterminate secondary causes cause, God makes use of all what it causes of being to achieve the divine intention for nature, by using it to create new instantiations of being. This divine providential action does not determine the outcome of the indeterminate natural activity (as in determining the outcome of the collapse of the wave function or how genes mutate), but by reaching effects that natural indeterminate causes cannot attain, referring to the second dynamic moment of God acting in and through natural agents. Thus, in the case of an event that was not determined in its cause but nevertheless happened, this event is also guided by the divine providence, because it is caused by God as its first cause, who causes everything that is of being in that event. By means of indeterminate natural causes, God causes what there is of being in this kind of events, in order to achieve the divine intention. As in the analogy of instrumental causality, in which the principal agent has goals that are not included in the causal power of the instrument, but which are nevertheless achieved, God reaches His goals, even when acting through contingent causes. In fact, although the *intentio* of the secondary cause does not extend to the indeterminate effect, God's intention does by ordering these new indeterminate effects to new good things in the universe.[82]

Perhaps surprisingly, Aquinas' theological and metaphysical notion of providence requires that the natural world include these kinds of indeterminate events. Even if Aquinas' arguments are of a metaphysical ilk rather than based on his knowledge of the natural world, contemporary Thomism can find some strong support offered by the natural sciences in this regard. For

---

[82] *SCG* III, c. 74.

Aquinas, a universe that includes all modes of being and of acting is more perfect than a universe that does not include one or more of these modes. One reads in his *Summa Contra Gentiles*: 'it would be against the perfection of the universe if there was nothing corruptible, or if no power would fail [in producing its effect]', quickly relating this idea with his doctrine of providence: 'it is against the notion of divine providence that there is nothing casual or random in things'.[83] For Aquinas a perfect universe, as per the definition of something perfect, is that which is complete. Hence, a complete universe, namely, that which includes all different modes of being and acting, is the most perfect universe. In fact, Aquinas repeatedly affirms not only that such a universe is more perfect, but that it is against the very notion of divine providence to affirm that there are no contingent, chanceful, or random events in it.[84]

Through the indeterminacies of nature, given that God acts in every single action of every single efficient cause as the primary cause of that action, and given that the actions of natural efficient causes can fail in the production of their effects, God can providentially reach new instantiations of being that would be better for the entire universe or a part of it. Thus, God guides the universe towards the end He determined by being the principal efficient cause using an instrument. So, not only did quantum indeterminacy allowed Thomists for offering a fuller account of their own doctrine of providence, but it also offers empirical support for an essential dimension of this doctrine.

4 Cosmology

The past century has been exciting for cosmology and as such it has presented several themes for Thomists upon which to reflect: Starting with the material formation of our world and the solar system in the early years of the twentieth century, through the proposal of the Big Bang beginning of the whole universe, to the challenge of multiverses and, closer to today, questions about life beyond Earth and its theological implications.

4.1 Early Cosmological Debates

Big Bang cosmology presented Thomism with a wide variety of possibilities of engagement about how the cosmos began to exist, but also, with later developments of the theory, about participatory theology, or how the cosmos participates in God's being. I shall discuss these paths in the following paragraphs, but

---

[83] *SCG* III, c. 74.

[84] Aquinas argues that 'if divine providence excluded all contingency, not all grades of beings would be preserved' (*SCG* III, c. 72), and that 'it would also be contrary to the character of divine providence if nothing were to be fortuitous and a matter of chance in things' (*SCG* III, c. 74). See Silva 2015.

first, it would be interesting to consider how early twentieth-century Thomists engaged with cosmological theories before the early developments of the Big Bang theory were presented in the works of Belgian priest and theoretical physicist George Lemaître (1894–1966) and American astronomer Edwin Hubble (1889–1953). Looking at some of these engagements would be a fruitful exercise for acknowledging that Aquinas' attitude of seriously considering the science of the time was passed to his disciples even almost seven centuries later and can continue to do so today.

Before Lemaître and Hubble suggested their ideas about the beginning of the universe, cosmological debates referred mostly to the so-called Laplace nebular hypothesis for the formation of the solar system. This hypothesis, originally developed in 1796, was widely discussed during the late nineteenth century and was not neglected in the Thomist philosophical and theological deliberations of the turn of the century. For Laplace, a protosolar cloud or nebula, in the process of cooling and contracting, flattened and spun more rapidly, shedding a series of gaseous rings of material, out of which the planets formed. This hypothesis was used by some Thomists as an opportunity to discuss the origin of the world as such.

For instance, in the first edition of his *magna opus* of 1899, the *Elementa Philosophiae Aristotelico-Thomisticae*,[85] one of the most widely used handbooks of Thomist philosophy throughout the twentieth century until the 1960s,[86] Gredt offers a succinct and simple description of the nebular hypothesis:

> there was a huge air-shaped sphere that revolved around its axis. Rings separated from this sphere by centripetal force, which were broken off by the force of attraction which they exerted on each other, and the parts, rising from thence, revolved around the central mass. These also took the form of spheres, from which again other spheres were detached by the same process. Thus, our solar system arose from masses broken up by the primordial nebula and later solidified. The other solar systems are also said to have evolved by a similar process.[87]

Gredt accepts as a matter of scientific discovery that our Solar System, as well as other solar systems in the universe, may have evolved according to this hypothesis, leaving the details of the explanation to the experts. Still, engaging philosophically with the theory, he claims that this nebular evolution could not have happened by a mere mechanistic process without any final cause at work, 'which at the beginning so directed the motion and combined the mass, that by the force of this primitive disposition it could have brought into being the

---

[85] Gredt 1899. [86] Elders 2020, 14. [87] Gredt 1899, 286.

most orderly system of the world'.[88] Now, to offer some demonstration of this thesis, Gredt presents two different arguments. The first one claims that the heavenly bodies are arranged among themselves in such a way that an ingenious and stable mechanism arises from them, affirming that 'the systems of the stars are arranged in such a way by a wonderful art, that disturbances which seem to arise in one side are compensated for in another; and it is contradictory for such an order to arise merely mechanically'.[89]

In the second argument Gredt suggests something like a proto fine-tuning argument or anthropic principle (or perhaps, a 'biotic principle') of sorts. He says:

> Our Earth is very neatly arranged so that it can be the home of living things, plants, animals, and human beings; but the Earth could not have arisen so arranged merely mechanically. In order for the Earth to be the place of living bodies, innumerable and very complex arrangements are required: 1) a fixed distance of the Earth from the Sun, a determined inclination of the ecliptic towards the equator, and other astronomical conditions; 2) a completely determined ground composition for the nutrition of plants; a determined mixture of gases, to serve for breathing, and innumerable other things, which could not arise purely mechanically.[90]

Out of these scientifically informed philosophical comments he obtains a theological rather telling conclusion: 'if in reality, as experts in natural things probably hold, the world arose out of a certain primitive nebula by way of evolution, this fact strongly speaks of the divine wisdom, which produced the world most artfully, the most beautiful of works of art; and in producing it used secondary causes'.[91]

In subsequent editions of his work, Gredt further developed his argument, engaging more with the scientific knowledge of his time and dropping his argument against mechanicism. He claimed that, even if the origin of the world most probably happened via evolution and that this origin is described with certain probability by Laplace's hypothesis, 'no cosmic evolution can be reasonably defended, except by admitting that from the beginning there was a most artful *teleological tension* in the primitive nebula'.[92] Interestingly, in a set of nested syllogisms to demonstrate the existence of this 'teleological tension' at the early stages of the universe, Gredt refers to his discussion about entropy and the dissipation of energy: if energy remains constant but dissipates, he argues, it must have been in greater tension at the early stages of the development of the nebula. Perhaps even more interesting, these nested

---

[88] Gredt 1899, 287. [89] Gredt 1899, 287. [90] Gredt 1899, 287. [91] Gredt 1899, 287.
[92] Gredt 1946, 280.

arguments also make reference to his earlier proto fine-tuning or biotic principle. What Gredt did in this particular case was attempting at understanding and explaining philosophically how the solar system was formed according to the science of his time. For doing so, he started in 1899 by postulating a teleological principle that guided the original dust cloud into forming spinning discs to form the Sun and the planets. By 1946, however, he realised that he could refer to a scientific principle, that of entropy and the dissipation of energy, to further explain this natural teleology within the physical system.

Writing at the same time, Édouard Hugon also engaged with Laplace's hypothesis, though with a different philosophical attitude: rather than looking at the science for tools to use in his metaphysical analysis of the formation of the solar system, Hugon employs the science as a door to speak about the divine nature. After presenting a classically Thomist account of creation ex nihilo, Hugon analyses this hypothesis affirming that it is 'most probably' the best way to explain the origin of the Solar System. In fact, he adamantly calls all (Thomist) philosophers not to disapprove of it. When confronted with the question of its relation to God, in a similar statement to that of Gredt, he calmly claims that 'if it is admitted that God created the first mass, and that he gave it the impulse and the power by which it could evolve, it implies nothing [repulsive for philosophers]'. In fact, in a theological comment he added that 'the power of God shines most clearly in this', since it shows that God 'is capable of bringing out innumerable and diverse masses from a single mass' as it also shows God's 'wisdom and goodness'.[93] Hugon was, in a way, prefiguring the type of engagement that many Thomists today have with Big Bang cosmology: rather than asking theological questions to the natural sciences, as Gredt seems to have done in this case, Thomists today usually reflect philosophically or theologically on the scientific theory to speak about God's nature and to portray in better ways Aquinas' doctrine of creation.

4.2 Big Bang Cosmology

In 1927, the very same year in which Werner Heisenberg proposed his uncertainty principle, George Lemaître published his work on an expanding universe, sourcing Friedmann models and relating them for the first time to the available observations of expansion of the Universe. This application led Lemaître to postulate the initial state of the universe in a primeval atom out of which the whole universe arose. A few years later in 1931, he described this cosmogonic evolution in these terms:

---

[93] Hugon 1905, 80.

we could conceive the beginning of the universe in the form of a unique atom, the atomic weight of which is the total mass of the universe. This highly unstable atom would divide in smaller and smaller atoms by a kind of super-radioactive process. Some remnant of this process might ... foster the heat of the stars until our low atomic number atoms allowed life to be possible.[94]

Just in the mid-year between these two, in 1929, Edwin Hubble suggested what was later known as Hubble's Law and today as Hubble-Lemaître Law, which describes in mathematical form the expansion of the universe referring to the fact that galaxies move away from each other proportionally to their respective distances. That is, the farther galaxies are, the faster they move. That 'super-radioactive' process of which Lemaître spoke to describe the initial state of the early universe is today referred as the initial big bang that originated the whole universe as we know it today. Thus, Lemaître's and Hubble's work set the observational basis for today's Big Bang theory.

This theory, speaking about the very origin of the whole universe, allowed new space for recovering the Thomistic doctrine of creation out of nothing. Following on the footsteps that the very Lemaître started, American Thomist philosopher William E. Carroll has made an important distinction between origins and beginnings.[95] The former refers to the ontological dependence to which Aquinas' doctrine of creation points, while the latter refers to the possible temporal commencement of the universe. 'Origins' speaks of a metaphysical discourse that surpasses the scientific discourse, while beginnings, by their very temporal nature, are knowable by the natural sciences. What Carroll suggests is that the beginning of the universe as we know it is something that falls within the remit of science, while its ontological origin must be studied and found within metaphysics. Furthermore, Carroll claims that it does not matter for the Thomist versed in metaphysics whether cosmology finds that the universe has infinite past, as the universe was thought to be prior to the Big Bang theory, or whether it has a discrete beginning, like Lemaître and Hubble described. As Carroll explains, 'there is no contradiction in the notion of an eternal, created universe: for were the universe to be without a beginning it still would have an origin, it still would be created'.[96]

The British Thomist theologian Andrew Davison is of similar ideas. Directly engaging with Stephen Hawking's ideas about the Big Bang, Davison strongly affirms that 'cosmological accounts of origins do not dispense with God, however, or with theology, since they offer no description of the origin of being qua being'.[97] Davison, as Carroll, finds the reason for this on an analysis

---
[94] Lemaître 1931, 706.
[95] Carroll 2012. See also another recent treatment of this topic in Tabaczek 2024.
[96] Carroll 2012, 144. [97] Davison 2018b, 379.

of Aquinas' notion of *creatio ex nihilo*, which means that 'God is *creator omnium*: the maker of all things, of every kind, in their entirety'.[98] Thus, '*creatio ex nihilo* also entails a prohibition on thinking of God as a cause among causes, or as a thing among things'.[99] And if this is the case, Davison concludes, 'our empirical observations will not apprehend him [God] as such; God is not a cause among causes, to be observed as such. Whatever we can see of creation will be creaturely'.[100]

4.3 The Multiverse

As a matter of fact, Carroll further explains, were our universe part of a multiverse like the one that Stephen Hawking described in his final years or of any other sort, the metaphysical claim would remain: 'Speculations that our universe is but one among a vast multiverse system may appeal to the imaginations of mathematical cosmologists like Stephen Hawking, but such speculations do not call into question the fact that whatever is, in whatever way or ways it is, is caused to be by God.'[101] After all, cosmology does not directly address the metaphysical and theological questions of creation. The philosophical notion of creation I have explained earlier, which implies a fundamental dependence of everything upon God for their very existence, does not in itself imply that all things have a temporal beginning: it simply points towards the constant giving of being by God to all existing things.

Italian theologian Giuseppe Tanzella-Nitti is of a similar idea, and develops it further, even suggesting that 'Thomas Aquinas addresses this question *ante litteram* in an article of his *Summa Theologiae*. Although within a very different conceptual framework than from the contemporary one, Aquinas concludes that one or more universes, as contingent beings, always need a causal origin from a Creator, Someone who is necessary in Himself'.[102]

This important development helps the philosopher, the scientist, and the theologian to avoid misunderstandings. 'It is the failure to recognize that to be created does not necessarily entail a temporal beginning that causes considerable confusion in contemporary debates about the implications of cosmology for arguments about whether or not the universe is created.'[103] Recognising this distinction between ontological origin and temporal beginning avoids such confusion. Again, the very engagement of the Thomist with a particular natural science, cosmology in this case, allowed for an important clarification of a metaphysical notion that has a direct implication on our understanding both the world and the divine nature.

---

[98] Davison 2018b, 372. [99] Davison 2018b, 372. [100] Davison 2018b, 373.
[101] Carroll 2012, 146. [102] Tanzella-Nitti 2022, 337. [103] Carroll 2012, 145.

Developing further Carroll's ideas about the multiverse, Jamie Boulding has recently published a study connecting the metaphysics of participation and cosmology, engaging with different authors, among whom Aquinas is present.[104] Boulding directly faces the question surrounding the metaphysical relations between the one and the many, a question that has been central to the whole history of philosophy, to tackle the implications that theories of the multiverse might have for theological discourses. Although Boulding analyses Plato and Nicholas of Cusa in addition to Aquinas, I shall focus on the latter. Boulding's main insight is that, if one looks at the multiverse through the lens of participatory ideas, it should not be conceived as an alternative to ideas of the divine, but rather as a manifestation of the divine infinitude and greatness. That is, a metaphysics and theology of participation shows that theological claims about the existence of a transcendent God are not at odds with a cosmic multiverse: 'Participation defines and governs the diverse ways in which different beings in a complex cosmic order can share in God's existence ... which is the only thing holding everything else in existence.'[105]

In his analysis of Aquinas, Boulding offers an example of this theological attitude when exploring ideas of cosmic and divine beauty. For many, including contemporary theologians such as Keith Ward and Rodney Holder, a multiverse is extravagant, uneconomical, far too complex, and implausible, while the idea of God as an explanation of the origin of our universe is simpler and more rational. Following on Aquinas' metaphysics of participation, however, Boulding shows that the diversity of the multiverse could be considered as an expression of God's infinite beauty and goodness, which no single creature is able to represent in its full: 'While God's being is simple and one and perfectly beautiful, it is received in creation in many diverse and varied ways. As such, God's beauty is expressed in creation in a diverse manner, and perhaps this will be further illustrated in the context of a tremendous diversity of cosmic realms.'[106] For Boulding, ultimately, participatory metaphysics can open a path to cosmologists to relate their own scientific theories to theological discourses. He presents another example when analysing Don Page's 'reflections on the cosmic diversity implied by string theory'.[107] These reflections are specifically theological, since Page considers the implications of string theory on his image of God. As such, Boulding suggests that when reflecting theologically, Page the scientist would be enlightened by resourcing some of Aquinas' ideas on participation, particularly those about beauty and diversity. Thus, Aquinas supplements Page's approach. Boulding presents several such

---

[104] Boulding 2022. [105] Boulding 2022, 94. [106] Boulding 2022, 106.
[107] Boulding 2022, 105.

examples of how participation could open paths to consider multiverse theories in a positive and creative relation to theological discourse. In his own words, a 'participatory cosmos can come into constructive interaction with the multiverse hypothesis and in unexpected ways might be more consistent with the implications of this hypothesis than is often assumed in contemporary theology, philosophy, and science'.[108]

4.4 Astrobiology

Andrew Davison has opened the doors for reflecting upon a new theme from the perspective of Thomism.[109] The discovery of habitable exoplanets has given a tremendous impulse to the consideration of the possibility of living beings in them. In fact, considering that life began on Earth quite early after its formation, it seems implausible to affirm that this is the only planet with such a phenomenon.

Among the many questions Davison addresses, the basic ones could be summarised in two: (1) whether extra-terrestrial life (including intelligent life) poses any challenge to a Christian understanding of creation; (2) whether intelligent extra-terrestrial life would require a different history of salvation.

Starting form Aquinas' notion of creation ex nihilo as the complete dependence of all being upon God and of the infinite perfection of God's being participated onto creatures, Davison recognises the full value of the whole of the universe, even of inanimate matter, since 'nothing that exists fails to participate in God'.[110] Still, given that there are degrees of being, from matter, through plants, to animals and human beings, Davison is 'warmly disposed' to acknowledging that 'additional species ... would expand the fullness of creation's capacity to reflect divine perfection in a creaturely way'.[111] So, given that creation is always lacking in displaying the perfection of the Creator, Davison argues that more living species might display more of that divine perfection.

This does not say much, yet, on the question about intelligent living beings somewhere beyond Earth. Their existence might seem to undermine the traditional understanding of human beings as the peak of creation. Still, considering the idea of *imago Dei*, Davison suggests that this notion should not be considered in competitive or comparative terms, arguing that the image of God could be shared among different material rational species. From a participatory perspective, Davison expects that 'the realisation of the image to be multifaceted precisely because it is an image of the infinite'.[112] This means, ultimately,

---

[108] Boulding 2022, 157. [109] Davison 2023. [110] Davison 2023, 79.
[111] Davison 2023, 86. [112] Davison 2023, 86.

that human beings are not 'the only creatures in the cosmos that could possesses' the image of God,[113] concluding that 'different rational creatures could possess diverse forms of finite intelligence',[114] since 'human beings do not exhaust what it means to bear even one aspect of the *imago dei*'.[115] In fact, as Davison points out, Aquinas does speak of different rationalities, in the broad sense, when considering angels, and even rational material beings when considering whether the celestial bodies moved by spiritual intelligences were rational beings.[116]

This acknowledgement of the possibility of other rational beings across the cosmos flings the doors wide open to theological considerations about the need for their salvation. Davison advocates for the possibility of unfallen rational beings beyond Earth, but he too considers the theological consequences of another fallen species beyond our planet, and whether the human history of salvation would be sufficient for their redemption. In his reply, Davison creatively follows Aquinas' teachings. First, since God could have saved the whole of humanity without becoming incarnate in Christ, Davison suggests that a 'theology of a single Incarnation in the entire cosmos could generally quite easily stretch to take in and affect species elsewhere'.[117] However, if 'Christ's example is the essence of his saving work, then multiple Incarnations may provide a better alternative'.[118] Now, Aquinas certainly allowed for the possibility of multiple Incarnations of any of the three persons of the Trinity as long as the nature that is being assumed has certain dignity, such as being rational (see questions 3 and 4 of the third part of the *Summa Theologiae*).[119] In relation to the *dignity*, Davison argues that even if Aquinas explicitly claims that only human nature is assumable, one should not exclude the possibility that extraterrestrial beings, which Aquinas did certainly not have in mind, might fulfil the criteria of rationality.[120] Thus, were there more than one rational material species in the universe, Davison is prone to accept the possibility of different incarnations in different species.

The basic argument for holding this position is as follows. Davison posits that, being human, Christ is the perfect human being, but 'no finite embodiment of God exhausts divine plenitude',[121] something to which Aquinas would agree. Thus, if there were multiple Incarnations in multiple rational species, in the same way as Jesus 'is what it means for God to have united human nature to

---

[113] Davison 2023, 163. [114] Davison 2023, 166. [115] Davison 2023, 168.
[116] Davison 2023, 182. [117] Davison 2023, 223. [118] Davison 2023, 223.
[119] Pawl 2016, 367, has summarised Aquinas' position regarding multiple incarnations with the following statement: 'There could be three simultaneously existing concrete rational natures, each of which is assumed by all three of the Divine Persons, at the same time.'
[120] See Davison 2023, 294. [121] Davison 2023, 265.

himself ... a Martian Christ would be what it means for God to have united a Martian nature to himself'.[122]

What is more, Davison shows that one of the important things for Aquinas about the Incarnation was that it was about establishing friendship between God and humanity. In fact, if Incarnation is only a means to redemption, then one should be enough. However, Incarnation is about God 'coming among us as one of us, drawing us into the mode of love known as friendship',[123] and in that respect Incarnations in other species would allow for God to make friends with them, as God did with human beings. Indeed, for Davison, 'one Incarnation could redeem the whole cosmos',[124] but it might be fitting for God to become incarnate in other rational species as to become friends with them.[125]

It is worth mentioning that not all Thomists agree with the possibility of multiple Incarnations. Tanzella-Nitti, for instance, suggests that 'theology can affirm reasonably that it is not by multiplying incarnations or sacrifices of the cross that the headship of Christ, the Incarnate Word, achieves cosmic meaningfulness and becomes more intelligible'.[126] Since the mystery of Incarnation is neither geocentric nor anthropocentric, but Christocentric, 'the Paschal Mystery of Christ possesses universal revelatory and salvific value'.[127]

For Tanzella-Nitti

> the 'absolute' character of what Christians believe happened on Earth in the person of Jesus of Nazareth does not depend on whatever importance a specific biological species might hold in the eyes of God ... It depends rather on the importance of the salvific decision through which the Creator Logos of the universe ... desired to become flesh, that is, a 'creature' in the womb of Mary, who is the womb of a people experiencing a specific salvation history.[128]

Given that Jesus calls for all peoples of every nation to participate in His mystery, *Tanzella-Nitti continues*, 'any intelligent creature ... all participate in the mystery of the Incarnate Word because they are creatures'.[129]

Be it one way or another, Christian theology is 'considerably more robust in meeting any confirmation of exobiology than is often assumed',[130] as Davison affirms by the end of his volume.

5 Evolutionary Biology

Evolutionary biology is perhaps the topic that disrupted the most the Thomistic school of thought, built throughout seven centuries of uninterrupted reflexion on

---

[122] Davison 2023, 267. [123] Davison 2023, 311. [124] Davison 2023, 313.
[125] Davison 2023, 365. [126] Tanzella-Nitti 2022, 317. [127] Tanzella-Nitti 2022, 315.
[128] Tanzella-Nitti 2022, 316. [129] Tanzella-Nitti 2022, 316. [130] Davison 2023, 365.

Thomas Aquinas' writings. Ever since Charles Darwin published his *On the Origin of Species* in 1859, Thomist scholars have followed different strategies to deal with the perceived downfall of teleological processes in the natural world. Of the very many questions that Darwin's theory poses to a Thomist view of nature, which include the problem of the apparition of human beings, their body and intelligence, as well as their capacity for love, the one that has most attracted the attention of Thomist scholars was that of the origin of living species in general.

A complete list of names within Thomism is virtually impossible to produce. Still, some of the scholars who engaged in their works with the theory of evolution in particular are, in a broad birth chronological order (with an attempt to cover all major Western geographical areas), Zeferino González y Díaz Tuñón, OP (1831–1894),[131] Charles Coppens, SJ (1835–1920),[132] Tilmann Pesch, SJ (1836–1899),[133] Michaele de Maria, SJ (1837–1913),[134] Bernard Boedder, SJ (1841–1917),[135] Juan José Urráburu, SJ (1844–1904),[136] Albert Farges (1848–1926),[137] Joseph Pohle (1852–1922),[138] Henry de Dorlodot (1855–1929),[139] Ambroise Gardeil, OP (1859–1931),[140] Juan González Arintero, OP (1860–1928),[141] Antonin Sertillanges, OP (1863–1948),[142] George Hayward Joyce, SJ (1864–1943),[143] Thomas Pègues, OP (1866–1936),[144] Édouard Hugon (1867–1929),[145] Joseph Donat, SJ (1868–1946),[146] Joseph de Tonquédec, SJ (1868–1962),[147] Stanislas-Alfred Lortie (1869–1912),[148] Karl Frank (1875–1950),[149] Jacques Maritain (1882–1973),[150] José Hellín, SJ (1883–1976),[151] Étienne Gilson (1884–1978),[152] Henri Collin (1888–1979),[153] Régis Jolivet (1891–1966),[154] Angelo Pirotta (1894–1956),[155] François-Joseph Thonnard (1896–1974),[156] Henri Grenier (1899–1980),[157] H.D. Gardeil, OP (1900–1974),[158] Stanislas Cantin (1901–1972),[159] André Munier,[160] Emmanuel Doronzo (1903–1976),[161] Charles de Koninck (1906–1965),[162] R.P. Phillips,[163] Leovigildo Salcedo, SJ (1909–2003),[164] Andreas Gerardus Maria van Melsen (1912–1994),[165] Henry Koren, CSSp (1912–2002),[166] Raymond J. Nogar (1916–1967),[167] Jean-Marie Aubert (1916–1994),[168] John Deely (1942–2017),[169] among many others.

---

[131] González 1873 and 1886. [132] Coppens 1891. [133] Pesch 1897. [134] Maria 1913.
[135] Boedder 1891. [136] Urráburu 1894. [137] Farges and Désiré 1921. [138] Pohle 1917.
[139] Dorlodot 1921 and 2009. [140] Gardeil 1893, 1894, 1895, and 1896.
[141] González Arintero 1898. [142] Sertillanges 1945. [143] Hayward Joyce 1922.
[144] Pègues 1927. [145] Hugon 1905. [146] Donat 1934. [147] Tonquédec 1918.
[148] Lortie 1917. [149] Frank 1926. [150] Maritain 1967. [151] Hellín 1950.
[152] Gilson 2009. [153] Collin 1926. [154] Jolivet 1940. [155] Pirotta 1936.
[156] Thonnard 1950. [157] Grenier 1944. [158] Gardeil 1966. [159] Cantin 1948.
[160] Munier 1956. [161] Doronzo 1968. [162] de Koninck 1961 and 2008.
[163] Phillips 1964. [164] Salcedo 1952. [165] Melsen 1965. [166] Koren 1955.
[167] Nogar 1963. [168] Aubert 1965. [169] Deely 1973.

This tradition continues today in the works of many contemporary scholars, such as William E. Carroll,[170] Juan Eduardo Carreño,[171] Edward Feser,[172] Simon Kopf,[173] Nicanor, Austriaco, OP,[174] and Mariusz Tabaczek, OP.[175] A quick survey of these authors and the titles of their works presents two tightly related traditions within Neo-Thomism, namely, a handbook and a research-oriented tradition – the former being an attempt at presenting the whole of Aquinas' ideas as a system in which evolutionary doctrines could or could not be accommodated; the latter having as its goal to rethink Aquinas' teaching in light of the scientific theories of evolution.

In this section I will present but a few thinkers and their ideas, starting with Neo-Thomists from the late nineteenth century until the early years of the twentieth century, moving on to the thought of two important Thomist scholars of the mid twentieth-century, and ending in some contemporary takes on evolution. The ideas of many will remain in their own pages; I hope this quick survey serves as a first step to engage with the school as a whole for many.

5.1 First Reactions

By the early years of the twentieth century, Édouard Hugon expressed in a widely read handbook that even if one could metaphysically hold that species had their origin through an evolutionary process guided by God, he preferred a kind of direct productionism, given some theological considerations about the beauty of the universe.[176] Not every Neo-Thomist, however, was of this idea, even if most rejected an atheistic take on evolution.

To the best of my knowledge, it was Spanish Dominican Zeferino González y Díaz Tuñón the Thomist who first engaged with Darwin's theory of evolution in the first Spanish edition of his *Filosofía Elemental* of 1873 (the topic was not included in the 1868 first Latin edition, though it was present in later editions). This should come as no surprise, since González always conversed with the sciences contemporary to him, such as phrenology, geology, and even the nascent palaeontology.[177]

For González, Darwin's theory was plainly false,[178] and it had 'a very close affinity with materialism and atheism, towards which it gravitates, if it is not identified with them'.[179] For his objections to the theory from a scientific perspective, he follows quite closely the ideas of Jean Louis Armand de Quatrefages (whom many Neo-Thomist would follow in subsequent years), a French biologist who strongly opposed Darwinian evolution by natural

---

[170] Carroll 2000. [171] Carreño 2024b. [172] Feser 2019. [173] Kopf 2023.
[174] Austriaco 2020. [175] Tabaczek 2023c. [176] Hugon 1905. See Silva 2024a.
[177] González 1864 and 1891. [178] González 1873, 289. [179] González 1886, 278.

selection. Still, for González, the most important objection was that Darwinism 'contains essentially anti-Christian doctrines',[180] in particular the idea that the human being could have evolved from primitive apes.[181] In what is perhaps a subtle blow against St. George Jackson Mivart (1827–1900), who just two years earlier had published his *On the Genesis of Species* offering a conciliation between Catholic doctrine and Darwin's theory,[182] González concludes that 'those who claim to reconcile Darwinism with Christianity give reason to suspect that they do not know either the former or the latter thoroughly'.[183] González worked with the first French translation of Darwin's *On the Origin of Species*, by Clémence Royer, from 1862, and quotes her systematically in this work to show this incompatibility.

A few years after this volume, however, González accepts a kind of moderate transformism with many restrictions, setting the scene for future Thomists:

> If we ignore the essentially atheistic-materialistic developments and applications; if we limit ourselves to the evolution or transformation of plant and animal species, which is what constitutes the fundamental and truly characteristic idea of Darwin's Darwinism; if from this Darwinism we also exclude its application to man, an application which science does not justify in any way, and if the appropriate reservations are made about the creation of the world and the rational soul, it can fit into Catholic dogmas.[184]

Tilmann Pesch, SJ, was an important German Thomist who also devoted much thought to the theory of evolution in the late nineteenth century. In his *Institutiones Philosophiae Naturalis*, Pesch affirms that the basic error Darwin and his followers make is to deny final causes.[185] Thus, he claims that 'the theory, according to which all organisms are said to have descended from some primitive organisms through continuous and gradual transmutation, cannot be admitted under any circumstances'.[186] In fact, since for him species are immutable, a tenet as the basis of all his argument, he also holds to be false that 'more perfect species of living things are said to have simply arisen from other, more imperfect species'.[187]

He is quick to affirm, however, that one should not be absolutely opposed to any kind of theory of transformation, only to those that hold that species come from other species absolutely speaking: 'Our thesis is put forward against any theory of descent, but not against any system of transformation'.[188] In fact, he suggests that species could undergo divinely guided transformations from less perfect to more perfect states, or even that God could use lower species to

---

[180] González 1873, 298. [181] González 1873, 298. [182] Mivart 1871.
[183] González 1873, 298. [184] González 1886, 285. [185] Pesch 1880, 75–76, 81–82, and 651.
[186] Pesch 1880, 624. [187] Pesch 1880, 655. [188] Pesch 1880, 658.

produce higher species 'so that He either implanted in this species the vital principle of the immediately superior species, or placed in it as it were higher germs, or produced in it the ovules of the superior species'.[189] So, in an argument that was later on closely followed by Hugon, Pesch finds three kinds of possible origins for living species: (1) the theory of production, which teaches that the Author of the world produced each species from inorganic matter; (2) the theory of descent *secundum quid*, which teaches that the Author of the world used lower species in producing higher species; (3) the theory of transformation, which teaches that there were interspecific transformation from lesser perfect to more perfect states.[190] Of all these, he prefers, as Hugon, productionism, though he admits that transformism and descent *secundum quid* could also be held with certain probability.

Spanish Dominican Juan José Urráburu was another deeply influential late nineteenth-century Thomist who devoted many a page to Darwin's theory. In his main work, the *Institutiones Philosophicae*, an eight-volume handbook that covers the whole of Thomistic philosophy, he devotes about three hundred pages to analyse and refute the 'atheistic and universal transformism'. For Urráburu, this theory was atheistic simply because, as it was presented, it denied the necessity of calling on God to guide the origin of new species on Earth, relying only in matter and its laws: 'therefore, the atheist transformism posits matter as infected and eternal, which, modifying itself from eternity according to the laws and powers inherent in it, takes on various successive forms ..., without intervening in this whole series of evolutions any powers or efficacies distinct from the uncreated matter itself'.[191]

The major problem for Urráburu was the evolution of man. For him, 'even if the doctrine of transformism could be admitted in other living species, it cannot be extended at all to explain the bestial origin of man',[192] even negating Mivart's innovative thesis – for that time – that the body of the human being could have evolved from previous species while the human soul could be created directly by God.[193] Still, after negating the possibility of the evolution of man, Urráburu spends much of what is left of his treatise to argument against the very theory of evolution with philosophical as well as scientific arguments. Among many of these arguments, Urráburu, in a paradigmatic Thomistic fashion, refers to the idea of natural teleology, explaining that 'the transformation of species, if it were possible, would occur from an innate tendency [to transform], as evolutionists teach ..., ' but this cannot be affirmed 'because such an innate tendency of a species to transformation is repugnant to nature ... no species or essence can

---

[189] Pesch 1880, 657.   [190] Pesch 1880, 675.   [191] Urráburu 1894, 330.
[192] Urráburu 1894, 394.   [193] Urráburu 1894, 415.

tend to an essential transformation without at the same time tending to its own destruction. But no nature tends to its own destruction, but to the preservation of its own being; for destruction is the evil of a thing, but its preservation is the good of nature'.[194] From this, and many other arguments, Urráburu concludes that 'each species originally needed the extraordinary influence of God'.[195]

Joseph Gredt, following Pesch, was more aligned with most Thomist authors writing during the first half of the twentieth century. In his 1899 *Elementa Philosophiae Aristotelico-Thomisticae*, he offered a simple, but fairly accurate, presentation of Darwin's theory of evolution by natural selection and random mutation, in which he stressed the absence of any teleology in the theory. Given this lack of any teleological element, Gredt dismisses Darwinism as false. Among the different arguments, he suggests that the distinction between species and varieties remained a problem, since varieties differed among themselves only accidentally, while species do so essentially. This difference does not allow for Darwinism to be true. To support this conclusion, Gredt explains, first, that there are abrupt changes between species and only gradual changes between varieties. Second, that since it is not evident that there are innumerable forms of species as Darwin predicted, because varieties do not move beyond the limits of the species, the latter are immutable, while the former are not. Third, that the innumerable intermediate forms, by which Darwinist join different species together, are not found either among the living or in the strata of the earth. Finally, that Darwin's law of inheritance is postulated too generally since the transmission of new features to posterity only occurs imperceptibly.

Even if he rejected Darwinism as such, Gredt did not want to commit to any sort of creationist position such as the one to which Pesch and Hugon held, suggesting that some kind of polyphyletic intra-species evolution could occur, which would give place, over different geological ages, to new more perfect forms of living beings (though not to new species). This type of evolution would be led by a teleological intrinsic tendency according to which the diverse types of a single species form. In fact, Gredt sees this intra-specific evolution as convenient to the Catholic faith since it allows avoiding God's repeated direct intervention.[196]

This requirement, namely, that God should act through secondary causes rather than having discrete interventions to create new species, motivated many other Thomists throughout the twentieth and twenty-first centuries. Désiré Mercier, for instance, writing also at the turn of the century, had a positive

---

[194] Urráburu 1894, 502. [195] Urráburu 1894, 586. [196] Gredt 1899, 293.

take on Darwin's theory of evolution. He presented his most detailed analysis in his autograph 1888 *Cours de Philosophie selon S. Thomas d'Aquin. La Psychologie*. His guiding intuition is that the facts on which the theory of evolution is based should fit into a teleological explanation. Mercier presents his views on Darwin's theory opposing them to both atheist and creationist positions: 'Others, more reserved than the first [atheists], more aware of science and more sincerely respectful of its conquests than the second [creationists], bow to the grandeur in the Darwinian hypothesis while avowing its defects and its shortcomings.'[197] This consideration led him to suggest an evolutionary process guided by God's providential action.

In fact, for Mercier the succession of species is the most solid argument in favour of Darwinism. Comparing Darwin's explanation to creationism, Mercier claims that the 'disappearance of thousands and thousands of living species ... represents the lower stages through which nature had to pass following a law of slow and continuous evolution to form current species', acknowledging this process to be 'one of the most important cogs of universal order'.[198] Thus, Mercier categorically states that Darwin's theory of evolution provides an explanation of these natural facts, while 'the hypothesis of successive creations does not provide it in a way that satisfies the mind'.[199]

Still, Mercier finds it necessary to express the theory of evolution in theological terms and presents his own metaphysical reading of the evolutionary process. He thus affirms that 'if the production of an organism appropriate to its environment requires the coincidence of millions or billions of active causes, this coincidence cannot occur and repeat itself indefinitely through the ages without there being in nature a real principle of harmony or finality responding to the thought of the one by whom the order was conceived',[200] stating, then, the necessity of a teleological order guided by God. Offering a nuanced description of how God is involved in the production of new species, Mercier affirms that

> the formation of each new natural or specific type is not explained, according to us, by a direct intervention of Providence ... we represent Providence intervening only when the reciprocal actions of the secondary causes have produced in the existing types a natural disposition that calls for a specific hierarchically superior form, and we like to think that this direct action could usually have been limited to a modification imprinted on the reproductive germ.[201]

Thus, for Mercier, God would intervene at the germinal level of conception, to modify it and thus elevate a species into another.

---

[197] Mercier 1887–88, 179. [198] Mercier 1887–88, 168. [199] Mercier 1887–88, 170.
[200] Mercier 1887–88, 181. [201] Mercier 1887–88, 183.

5.2 Mid Twentieth-Century Thomism

By the mid-point of the twentieth century many a Thomist had already accepted the basic solution that, guided by God, animal species could have evolved in the long history of the Earth. This was the position that the Belgium priest Henry de Dorlodot had defended in his 1921 work *Le Darwinisme au point de vue de l'Orthodoxie Catholique* (translated into English a year later).[202] Dorlodot held something in between absolute evolutionism (without any divine input) and 'fixism' or 'creationism', affirming that the first life on Earth should have started with a direct divine act and that this primordial organism (or organisms) gave rise to the wide variety of living species over the centuries through the process of evolution: 'the Catholic theory concerning the natural operations of secondary causes is sufficient to account for a natural transformist evolution such as Darwin held'.[203]

This position extended to much of Catholic thought of the time. For instance, American philosopher Henry Koren, who would later be quite influential in the solution presented by Edward Feser these days, held that 'it does not seem impossible that the various species have developed from one or a few primitive types of organisms through the internal forces of nature as directed by God'.[204] Koren also suggested that the philosophical species which would transform were actually 'the inanimate, vegetative, sensitive, and rational',[205] from which other subspecies would form. This position was succinctly defended a couple of decades earlier by Charles de Koninck, in his 1936 essay *Le Cosmos*: 'The ensemble of beings constituting nature is divided into four species: men, animals, plants, and the inorganic ... These four species are the only ones philosophically definable. The canine species is not a species in the philosophical sense.'[206] Ultimately, for Koren, evolution within species would be reduced to accidental changes rather than substantial changes.

Jacques Maritain suggested something along these lines when he, in 1967, affirmed that with his doctrine of degrees of living beings, Aquinas offered 'basis of the philosophy of Evolution and the metaphysical principles of a truly evolutionist thought'.[207] The basic idea is that the order of ascending perfection in living things of which Aquinas speaks implies a general tendency towards higher degrees, that is, 'an aspiration towards the form of a higher metaphysical degree',[208] and 'if we add the dimension of time to this metaphysical tendency, it becomes an evolutionary tendency'.[209]

---

[202] Dorlodot 1922. [203] Dorlodot 1922, 105. [204] Koren 1955, 307.
[205] Koren 1955, 306. [206] de Koninck 2008, 258. [207] Maritain 1967, 94.
[208] Maritain 1967, 92. [209] Maritain 1967, 122.

Now, this tendency, in the case of the evolution of species, is supplemented by the efficient causality of the Cause of being, which works as 'a superelevating and superforming motion (I would like to be able to say "creative"), which is exercised by God as the first cause of the mutation which will pass from one species to another'.[210] For Maritain, 'the divine superelevating and superforming motion moves a living being to become – at least in its descendants – better than it is, so that in the prenatal life of the being engendered by it (still if it is an animal) the soul, first vegetative, then sensitive, educed from the power of matter is of a specific degree higher'.[211]

So, Maritain argues, there are two different causal sources of the evolution of the species: (1) the causality of the Creator of the being, and his superelevating and superforming motion; (2) 'the causality of the living itself, whose immanent activity, under the elevating motion of the First Cause, invents, by the self-regulating process proper to the living, something new which, first affecting the organism of the latter, will pass into the gonads and into the virtue of the generative act'.[212]

In his 1971 *D'Aristote à Darwin... et retour*, Étienne Gilson sets out to demonstrate that the notion of final causality, or teleology, is not a scientific notion, but rather a philosophical one (and not even a theological one), that, properly speaking, belongs to the philosophy of nature, and within this discipline to the philosophy of life.[213] In doing so, he hopes to show that a merely mechanical philosophical take on science is not enough, even if a philosophy of nature that acknowledges teleology can also include mechanical explanations. In what is perhaps the core of this work, Gilson shows how for Darwin himself the beauty of adaptations he had found in nature opened the path for speaking in teleological terms about nature, even if he did not do so explicitly in his works, or, what is most, even if he doubted this conclusion. Thus, Gilson affirms that 'the adaptation of an organism to its surroundings and to its conditions of existence, and those of parts of an organism to other parts of it, are intelligible only from the point of view of their final result'.[214]

This teleology, however, should not be understood in terms of an externally divinely imposed teleology that one can discover: 'the first and foremost error is to conceive of natural finality as the result of an intention first present in the thought of God and capable, consequently, if one discerns it, of explaining the structure of his work. This theological finality is that of which Charles Darwin is the sworn enemy'.[215] On the contrary, a philosophical notion of teleology that could be applied to evolutionary processes refers to an internal tendency to vary

---

[210] Maritain 1967, 121.   [211] Maritain 1967, 121.   [212] Maritain 1967, 123.
[213] Gilson 2009, 16.   [214] Gilson 2009, 88.   [215] Gilson 2009, 88.

spontaneously.[216] In this respect, 'the problem of final causality is unavoidable in the perspective of the evolution of species'.[217] In fact, as Gilson shows, Darwin expressed some sympathy to this idea when writing to Asa Gray, who had claimed that Darwin had returned teleology to natural science, and even Thomas Huxley was of a similar idea when claiming that beyond design, there was a wider teleology as the basis of the theory of evolution.[218]

5.3 Contemporary Thomist Engagements

Most of the late nineteenth- and early twentieth-century Thomist engagements with transformism and evolutionary theory have, in a way, paved the path for many more examples of contemporary Thomistic engagement with evolutionary process and God's place in it. Some of these later developments refer to the origin of the different living species, as in the past, but also to other challenges, such as those coming from the problem of evil and the consideration of the doctrine of original sin.

In his recent *Aristotle's Revenge*, American philosopher Edward Feser offers a rediscovery of teleology within the theory of evolution. In fact, he argues that even Darwin thought that the guiding mechanism for the transformation of species, namely, natural selection, could be seen as a teleological process. His main argument starts from an analysis of what he calls the 'selection for' problem, which basically states that, given that natural selection is blind and mindless, it cannot be said with certainty that it selects for some traits in particular or another, since the causal network that might lead one to claim that this trait was selected for would equally justify that this other one was actually selected for, and, thus, the theory would lose its causal explanatory power.[219] For Feser, 'given the assumption of metaphysical naturalism' in most current debates over teleology and evolution, there is no way to solve this problem, simply because of the non-teleological conception of nature that is held throughout these debates.[220] Nevertheless, if one recalls that there are at least two available distinct notions of teleology, Feser argues, one may solve the problem.

So Feser introduces at this point the notions of *intrinsic* and *extrinsic* teleology, the former referring to things or processes that have teleological features when 'those features follow from its very nature', while the latter refers to a thing or a process whose features 'are in no way intrinsic to it, but entirely imposed from outside', like time-telling for a watch.[221] Intrinsic teleology Feser terms *Aristotelian teleological realism*. He also refers to a third possibility,

---
[216] Gilson 2009, 89. [217] Gilson 2009, 92. [218] Gilson 2009, 90–91.
[219] Feser 2019, 410. [220] Feser 2019, 416. [221] Feser 2019, 416.

which he calls *Scholastic teleological realism*, which is 'a variation on the Aristotelian position . . . [that] takes the divine intellect to be the ultimate cause of things having the natures they do'.[222]

Now, if one assumes that God exists and holds the theory of evolution by natural selection to be plausible, then one has elements to solve the 'selection for' problem, since one may hold to a kind of intrinsic teleology that would disentangle the question. In fact, one may even hold an atheistic Aristotelian teleological realism, without committing to metaphysical naturalism, which, as Feser suggests, Darwin held to when affirming the existence of a kind of natural teleology connected to the operations of natural selection, in the sense that it is a tendency to select traits that are advantageous for survival.[223] Thus, Feser argues that rather than banishing teleology from biology, Darwin presupposed it, and that if one wants to be a Darwinian, one needs to be an Aristotelian.[224]

When discussing the possibility of the coming to be of some species from other species, Feser is clear that one could hold to the thesis within Thomism. Feser suggests utilising the notion of *philosophical species* which de Koninck and Koren had used previously, naming the four different kinds of things in an Aristotelian material world: inanimate things, plants, sentient things, and rational things. Within these one finds the different subspecies that fill this world. For instance, within sentient things, one finds reptiles, birds, mammals, and so on, as well as further subdivisions within them. The ultimate question is, then, whether one philosophical species could originate another philosophical species. If someone holds that the inanimate can originate all other philosophical species, then one holds to *universal transformism*. *Mitigated transformism*, on the contrary, holds that some transformations from one philosophical species to another are not possible.[225]

Within mitigated transformism, Feser points out two possibilities. First, one may hold that 'even though transformations between philosophical *sub*species are naturally possible, transformations between philosophical *species* are not, and would require special divine action'.[226] In this option, the inanimate cannot give place to the living, the vegetative cannot give place to the sentient, and the sentient cannot give place to the rational. Each of these steps would require a special creative act of God. Feser calls this possibility *Aristotelian theistic evolutionism*, as mitigated transformism that requires direct divine intervention at the most significant transitions.

The second possibility holds that 'even transformations between philosophical species are naturally possible and therefore would not require special divine

---

[222] Feser 2019, 417. [223] Feser 2019, 418–419. [224] Feser 2019, 420.
[225] Feser 2019, 428. [226] Feser 2019, 429.

action'.[227] This *Aristotelian natural evolutionism* would affirm 'either a universal transformism or near-universal transformism (if an exception is made in the case of human origins)' and posits 'a natural kind of evolution insofar as it holds that the transitions even between (all or most) philosophical species can occur without special divine action, just by virtue of physical substances exercising the causal powers that follow from their natures'.[228] Certainly, Feser discloses, an Aristotelian natural evolutionist could 'perfectly well hold that God is the cause of there being a world of inanimate physical substances with causal powers that evolutionally gave rise to a variety of vegetative and animal forms of life'.[229]

Mariusz Tabaczek holds to something of the like. He has recently published a profound metaphysical re-reading of the Thomist understanding of natural causes in light of evolutionary processes. Building on recent developments of essentialism in philosophy of biology, Tabaczek proposes understanding biological species in hylomorphical terms. In particular, Tabaczek highlights the role that the material cause has, given its intrinsic passive potency. In fact, it is this passive potency in natural things, being 'one of the most basic metaphysical principles underlying the very fabric of the universe',[230] that explains their capacity for evolving into other species, given the proper time and environmental circumstances: 'An evolutionary transition might be thus defined, in this account, as a series of minor genetic and epigenetic changes that effect minor phenotypic variations. These variations may become permanent, which, in turn, gradually changes the 'proximate disposition' of prime matter underlying subsequent organisms.'[231] In this account, Tabaczek emphasises,

> it takes many mutations and epigenetic changes (the outcome of which are regulated by natural selection) to produce such an effect (*i.e.*, the difference in kind between parents and their offspring), and its actual instantiation may be extremely difficult (if not impossible) to capture. But this does not exclude the possibility of its occurring, especially in a situation where some members of a species migrate to a new environment and can be modified gradually in subsequent generations, to the point where they can no longer mate with the other descendants of their ancestors.[232]

Having set the basis for a philosophical account of evolutionary theory, Tabaczek is careful to acknowledge that the transformation of one species into another is due to a highly complex set of causes that contribute to a multifaceted history of evolutionary transitions.[233]

---

[227] Feser 2019, 430. [228] Feser 2019, 430. [229] Feser 2019, 431.
[230] Tabaczek 2023c, 30. [231] Tabaczek 2023c, 34. [232] Tabaczek 2023c, 36.
[233] Tabaczek 2023c, 49.

Tabaczek, however, is not happy with only reformulating the metaphysical tools of Aquinas' natural philosophy in light of evolutionary processes. He moves into theological ground to affirm a model of theistic evolution in Thomistic terms, albeit one that would require 'introducing some adjustments to Aquinas' theological system'.[234] For Tabaczek, the novelty in things brought about through evolutionary processes does not actually require God's creative action. Instead, the apparition of new species should be understood in terms of God's providential guiding of the created nature, as a principal agent working through secondary and instrumental causes in actualising the unlimited potency of matter. Sourcing the metaphysical distinction between *essentia* (essence) and *esse* (existence), Tabaczek suggests that God would be the ultimate cause of a things' existence (in terms of its coming to be, its continuous existence, and of *esse* as such) and of a thing's essence (in terms of the first historical apparition of the essence as a new species from the potency of matter as well as the thing's essence as such); while creatures would be secondary causes of the coming to be of a new thing and its essence, and instrumental causes of another thing's essence and existence as such.[235]

Nicanor Austriaco addresses the challenge of the origin of human beings brought about by the theory of evolution through natural selection discussing the chanceful appearance of human language, an essential element of what a human being is, through a mutation in the *FOXP2* gene at some point in the last 200,000 years of human history. Austriaco sees in this happening an example of how God and nature are at work in random mutations. Austriaco explains that the mutation that 'gave rise to language use occurred when a particular DNA polymerase was repairing a DNA strand damaged by high energy radiation'.[236] Following a similar account to the one I offered previously, Austriaco holds that God can be seen to have acted as efficient cause in this event because God gives the DNA strand and the DNA polymerase their existence and their natures. Thus, the DNA polymerase can repair the DNA strand because God makes them what they are. This means that the DNA polymerase was able to introduce a random mutation into the *FOXP2* gene precisely because God made it to be contingent in its operation and, so, capable of making random mistakes. This random mistake followed the created contingent nature of the polymerase. Reflecting on the distinction between creaturely and divine activity, Austriaco argues that 'classical double agency allows one to accomplish the task of explaining noninterventionist objective special divine action without denying either the mystery of divine providence where God knows all events in past, present, and future, or the radical distinction between

---

[234] Tabaczek 2023c, 157.   [235] Tabaczek 2023c, 141.   [236] Austriaco 2003, 956.

the Creator and his creatures'.[237] Austriaco thus holds to this distinction that serves him to express the randomness and chanceful character of natural events as well as God's providence present in evolutionary processes.

William Carroll expands on and emphasises this distinction between creaturely and divine action through an in-depth analysis of the notion of creation, addressed earlier. For Carroll, 'the very processes which evolutionary biology explains depend upon God's creative act'.[238] Thus, the intelligibility of nature, which is described with certain accuracy by the natural sciences, 'depends upon a source which transcends the processes of nature', because 'without the very fact that all that *is* is completely dependent upon God as cause, there would be no evolution at all'.[239] The radical dependence of the natural world upon God both in its being and in its acting cannot be negotiated, and this dependence explains that nature is causally powerful. In fact, 'no matter how random one thinks evolutionary change is ... no matter how much one thinks that natural selection is the master mechanism ... the role of God as Creator, as continuing cause of the whole reality of all that is, is not challenged'.[240] Moreover, this relation of dependence implies that 'there would be no autonomy to the natural order were God not causing it to be so'.[241]

It is worth, also, mentioning at this point – at least in passing – a position that some contemporary Thomists hold in denying the possibility of interpreting Aquinas' philosophy and theology in an evolutionary key (as most do today and many, as I have shown, did in the past). Polish Dominican friar Michael Chaberek has been the champion of this position, strongly suggesting that there is an intrinsic contradiction between Thomism and the theory of evolution.[242] The basic claims are that, first, the lower cannot produce the higher, and thus, a lower species cannot produce the higher species; and second, that species are produced by creation only, given that Aquinas explicitly claims that the first of every species is created by God. The reason given for the latter is that, for Aquinas, any individual of a given species requires a parent of the same species for its generation.

As a preliminary objection to the first claim, one may suggest revisiting the idea that providence, in utilising secondary causes as instruments, can achieve effects that go beyond the causal power of the secondary cause, and so the claim that the lower cannot produce the higher looses meaning, as Tabaczek explains. The anti-evolutionist might counterargue with the second claim, that species are produced only by creation. To this, however, one may suggest that Aquinas held this position because he did not have at hand any other plausible natural

---

[237] Austriaco 2003, 950. [238] Carroll 2010, 51. [239] Carroll 2010, 51 (my emphasis).
[240] Carroll 2008, 591. [241] Carroll 2008, 595. [242] Chaberek 2017.

explanation. Now we do, with evolutionary theory. Regardless of my suggestions, Chaberek holds to the position of Intelligent Design and affirms that it is the closest to Aquinas' own position, something to which many within the school have objected. Notably among these are the works of Austriaco and Tabaczek.[243]

Andrew Davison has suggested that Thomists might be looking at the issue of the evolution of species from a misguided angle, and proposed looking at the doctrine of divine exemplars to dilute the challenge that the process of evolution might pose to the production of living species. For him, 'evolution has forced us to turn away from an account of creation that imagines God creating and forming the prototypes of species one by one and side by side'.[244] In this respect, the doctrine of divine exemplars as it is traditionally understood might be seen as in danger, since there are no permanent forms in things which resemble the divine perfections. Still, if one gives up on exemplars, Davison argues, one risks also leaving the doctrine of *creatio ex nihilo*, since that which is intelligible in created things, their natures, comes from the divine exemplars. Thus, the Thomist must offer a cogent account of exemplarity in face of an evolutionary nature. In what might be considered as surprising for many, Davison finds that 'Aquinas saw God as primarily the exemplar of *individual* creatures'.[245] Thus, 'if the divine ideas relate primarily to individuals, the change of species over time is no longer a problem'.[246]

In this sense, then, the diversity and mutability of species is secondary to what the individuals of a species share. For Davison, ultimately, 'in aligning divine exemplarity primarily with the individual creature, Aquinas very considerably opened the scope for relating that exemplarity to the variation of species over time'.[247] This means that, contrary to what would have been presumed, Darwinian evolution threatens in no way the doctrine of divine exemplarism. Instead, 'from an exemplarist position, evolution is fitting'.[248]

5.4 Other Contemporary Challenges: Evil and Original Sin

If the theory of evolution does not challenge the doctrine of exemplarity, it does pose another challenge that has recently become more prominent in scholarly circles, namely, that of animal suffering. This problem has been debated ever since Darwin wrote to Asa Gray that 'there seems to me too much misery in the world. I cannot persuade myself that a beneficent & omnipotent God would have designedly created the Ichneumonidæ with the express intention of their

---

[243] For more on this matter, see Austriaco 2017; Tabaczek and Chaberek 2024; Tabaczek 2022.
[244] Davison 2018a, 1101.   [245] Davison 2018a, 1078.   [246] Davison 2018a, 1079.
[247] Davison 2018a, 1080.   [248] Davison 2018a, 1081.

feeding within the living bodies of caterpillars, or that a cat should play with mice'.[249] There is, for Darwin, too much pain and suffering in the evolutionary process to account for a benevolent and omnipotent Creator. Ultimately, there is too much waste, too many species left to die, too much suffering in the animal kingdom has passed as to arrive at our present time. Evolution seems to be too ruthless of a natural process for it to allow for God. Though this is certainly more a problem pertinent to the philosophy of religion within the vast question of the problem of evil, it is an issue raised by evolutionary science, and so a few words on it are in order, as some Thomists have of late tackled it and offered some replies.

It is probably B. Kyle Keltz who has offered the most comprehensive Thomist reply to the problem of animal suffering.[250] His main argument relies mostly in Aquinas' view of evil as privation, which entails that animal suffering and pain is not evil, and thus the problem of evil is not amplified by considerations about the evolutionary development of life. Furthermore, Keltz argues that God is not obligated to create a world without animal suffering, since prior to creation there was nothing towards which God would have a duty. Ultimately, God is not moved by any kind of necessity in creating the world as it is or as it could have been any other way. Italo-Argentine philosopher Juan José Sanguineti further explains that 'arguments rejecting God's existence because of animal suffering ... often focus on the negativity of animal pain in such a way as to make it unintelligible'.[251] However, for Sanguineti, animal pain 'does not have the drama or the scope present in human experience. It does not have the drama produced by the intellectual awareness of one's pain and that of others, which makes one wonder about its meaning and thereby suffer for not understanding it'.[252] Keltz would agree in this point, affirming that 'animal suffering is not morally significant not only because nonhuman animals are arational, but also because they lack self-awareness'.[253]

In an interesting twist, both Keltz and Sanguineti show the power of Thomistic metaphysics and theology on this question by suggesting that for Aquinas there was animal suffering even before original sin. Sanguineti explains that, for Aquinas, physical nature before sin was not different from today's:

> It had the same laws and structures before and after the original sin ... Thomas disqualifies, the idea that, before the original fall, God would have created a different, 'more perfect' physical universe, excluding death or decompositions in the world of life. He rejects the claim that in the absence

---

[249] Darwin, Charles, 'Letter 2814' to Asa Gray on 22 May 1860, paragraph 3.
[250] Keltz 2020. [251] Sanguineti 2023, 6. [252] Sanguineti 2023, 6. [253] Keltz 2020, 36.

of the original sin animals would not have been fierce or kill, calling this opinion 'totally irrational'.[254]

The simple conclusion that Sanguineti extracts from this position is that 'there is no incompatibility between the thesis of original sin (and the previous state) and modern evolutionary biology',[255] at least within a Thomistic framework.

Keeping within this theological theme, Daniel W. Houck has offered a new reading of original sin from a Thomistic perspective in relation to the theory of evolution.[256] Following on Aquinas' teachings, Houck affirms that original sin should be understood as 'a privation of the gift of grace, not nature'.[257] The theory of evolution, however, poses at least two challenges to this theological doctrine: (1) the fact that the first human beings inherited tendencies towards sinful behaviour from their non-human predecessors or, said it positively, the fact that 'the doctrine of original justice requires that the first humans could have lived without the desire for sin';[258] (2) the fact that, according to contemporary evolutionary theory, 'human beings evolved as community of more than two people'.[259]

To the first, Houck suggests two possible solutions: (1) that 'the first humans were created in sanctifying grace which restrained all their disordered desires'; (2) that 'the first humans were created in sanctifying grace that did not restrain all their naturally disordered desires. The grace was sufficient to give them free will to resist these desires, however'.[260] For Houck the former is more difficult to hold together with evolutionary theory, though not impossible, while the latter is easier to square with evolution but is open to the objection that evil is built into creation. In this position, he leaves the question unresolved. Nicanor Austriaco decidedly prefers the first of these options, sourcing to the notion of 'preteradaptive gifts' – which he coined – to explain how the first human beings could have resisted such disordered desires inherited from their ancestors: 'it would also have been fitting for God to give the original human beings what I am calling the preteradaptive gifts to remedy and perfect those evolved adaptations that in themselves would have hindered human persons from attaining their beatitude in God'.[261]

To the second challenge brought about by evolutionary theory to the doctrine of original sin, namely, that human beings evolved in a community rather than

---

[254] Sanguineti 2023, 16. [255] Sanguineti 2023, 16. [256] Houck 2020.
[257] Houck 2020, 256. [258] Houck 2020, 185.
[259] Houck 2020, 189. There is one further challenge that Houck lists, referring to the possible alteration of the human DNA by the first sinful action. For Houck, however, the Thomist position 'does not claim that our DNA has been corrupted or altered' since original sin 'is not the loss of a "strictly natural" trait ... that was to be transmitted throughout the generations'. 2020, 204.
[260] Houck 2020, 205. [261] Austriaco 2015, 658.

individually, Houck, once again, offers two possibilities of solutions: one affirming the historicity of the Fall, the other, not committing to it. As for the first one, Houck presents the following scenario: 'the first human beings are created in grace. They sin and forfeit grace, and as a result they transmit sinful human nature to the next generation'.[262] As for the second, which is Houck's preferred option, he offers the following scenario: 'God can create a human being with only the principles of nature and what follows from them. Such a creature is oriented to God, not sinful self-love. But she needs grace to be saved. This, on my view, just is what it means to be in a state of original sin.'[263] As with the former case, Austriaco prefers the first option, affirming that 'an evolutionary perspective does not undermine this traditional account of human origins and original sin. In fact, I propose that reflecting upon both our evolutionary origins and our present psychological constitution in light of divine revelation reveals that the wounds of fallen human nature are still very real'.[264]

As it should be evident by now, all these authors, as so many others I did not include here, engaged with contemporary evolutionary theory taking it seriously and modelled their Thomistic metaphysical and theological accounts to it in one way or another. These engagements, certainly, do not intend to mix theological or metaphysical discourses with scientific ones. Far from it, they intend to take the science as it and relate it to a theological perspective of the world. In doing such, I see many of them as exemplars of science-engaged Thomism, present throughout the recent history of the school in its relation to evolution.

6 Further Developments

After this concise account of three of the most important encounters of Thomism with the natural sciences, I will present here a few more examples of current areas of exploration for engagement between the two. Due to space, I shall not get into the details of each of the topics I will present, but I think it is worth mentioning these as to show the vast spectrum of possibilities that science-engaged Thomism offers today.

6.1 The Human Soul and the Cognitive Sciences

Perhaps one of the most important of these is that of the human soul and the cognitive sciences. Some of the Neo-Thomists, much referred to in this Element, had already engaged with the psychology of their time to delve into the intellectual life of human beings. Such was the case of Désiré Mercier, who,

---

[262] Houck 2020, 207.   [263] Houck 2020, 207.   [264] Austriaco 2015, 664.

as was mentioned earlier, offered a big impetus to psychological studies in his philosophy institute in Louvain in the early twentieth century, to the point of integrating a psychological laboratory into his institute.

Closer to us today, Daniel de Haan is actively conversing with the new mechanical philosophy (NMP) in order to engage with the neurosciences, given its interest in the methods and practices of scientists searching for biochemical, genetic, neurophysiological, and psychological mechanisms. His first step is to argue that the new mechanical philosophy allows us to understand better the hylomorphic constitution of animals and their psychosomatic operations. On the one hand, the new mechanical philosophy suggests that there is a multilevel causal and explanatory pluralism at work in the sciences, just as a hylomorphic stance on natural things would also hold. In fact, the new mechanical philosophy has a 'realist account of organization as an irreducible ontological and explanatory factor in every mechanism',[265] that actually makes a difference with respect to the causal operations of the component entities it organises. Given these features, de Haan argues that the hylomorphic 'account of embodied psychological powers can accommodate and be enriched by NMP's presentation of mechanisms in biology, neuroscience, and psychology'.[266] In this sense, for instance, the psychosomatic power of vision 'enlist a coordinated manifestation of a complex range of psychosomatic powers or mechanisms that constitute the activity of seeing'.[267]

Now, because every animal's action is by its metaphysical composition hylomorphic and, thus, psychosomatic, 'there is no dichotomy between consciously seeing and the processes of the nervous system'.[268] Now the issue with intellectual operations of human beings is a bit different from sensory cognition, because intellectual operations, for Thomists, are not material, that is, they are not ontologically dependent on organic powers. Given the animality of human beings, however, these intellectual disembodied operations and powers are in constant interaction with all bodily cognitive capacities. So, de Haan's main question is 'how immaterial intellectual operations can interact with other psychological operations that are embodied in the nervous system'.[269]

The recourse to the new mechanical philosophy allows him to source other types of causal explanation to solve this conundrum, claiming that 'it is not mere efficient causality but formal and final causality that are critical for understanding the interaction between noetic operations and psychosomatic operations'.[270] That is, the intellectual disembodied operations of human beings with psychosomatic operations via formal and final causality ordering the manifestation of

---

[265] de Haan 2017, 19.   [266] de Haan 2017, 21.   [267] de Haan 2017, 16.
[268] de Haan 2017, 16.   [269] de Haan 2018, 56.   [270] de Haan 2018, 69.

psychosomatic powers.[271] Ultimately, this model saves the fact that the human person is one unity with a multiplicity of operations and actions: 'When a human person acts or is acted upon these activities enlist a panoply of noetic and psychosomatic powers – and the organized hierarchical complex of neural, biochemical, and physical subsystems that constitute psychosomatic powers – whose coordinated and integrated operations enable the human person to perform the activities in question.'[272]

6.2 Human Enhancement

A question also related to human nature is that of the possible enhancement of it, particularly its moral character. This question is directly related to the transhumanist movement, and it has sprung some interesting responses from contemporary Thomists. Perhaps the most important difference to which Thomists signal in contrast with their anthropological stance is the transhumanist quasi-dualist view in their search for transposing someone's mind into another substrate and thus seek immortality.[273] In this regard, the Thomist, as I have just shown, understands the human being as a unity of matter and form, body and soul, and hence, one's own soul could not be transplanted into a different body (be it by transplanting one's own brain into another human body or by uploading one's own mind into another material structure).

Regardless of this core difference, when confronted with the question of moderate enhancement of the human nature, Jason Eberl argues that 'a Thomistic Aristotelian account of human nature and flourishing may allow for, and perhaps even encourage, certain forms of enhancement',[274] as long as these enhancements are directed towards the proper end of human life, namely, flourishing.[275] Eberl offers some examples of such potentially permissible enhancements: 'increased memory capacity, a more robust immune system, alleviation of moderate social anxiety, and elimination of certain cognitive biases that contribute to poor practical reasoning and subsequent unethical behaviour'.[276] For Eberl, cognitive enhancements, such a technologically enhanced memory (which is 'a key component of our neurologically based cognitive architecture that is essential for intellective thought to occur'[277]) coheres with the Thomistic aim of flourishing by improving our rational powers in pursuit of truth and practical activities.

Similarly, physical enhancement could be sought as long as it benefits bodily health, and thus contributes to human flourishing, given that 'the bodily

---

[271] de Haan 2018, 75.   [272] de Haan 2018, 61.
[273] Eberl 2022, 80; Asla 2019; Tabaczek 2023b.   [274] Eberl 2022, 85.   [275] Eberl 2014, 290.
[276] Eberl 2022, 85.   [277] Eberl 2014, 300.

functions endemic to our essential animality are both intrinsically and instrumentally valuable by subserving our intellective activity'.[278] Moral enhancement is a bit more difficult to tackle, since it requires the human being to have a certain moral character before choosing enhancing it: 'certain forms of moral bioenhancement may assist those who already possess a basic inclination toward virtue, and an incipient degree of prudence already cultivated, either to become themselves or to help others become, even more virtuous by becoming more prudent moral reasoners'.[279]

The idea is that one should consider whether by assisting one's emotional response (such as patience) with a pill that helps achieve a desired virtuous action is leading the person to true flourishing or is a simple illusion. In Eberl's words,

> whether one is being helped to cultivate virtue through their own efforts of practical reasoning and psychological self-mastery or being offered a mere simulacrum of true moral virtue ... the risk of inauthentic cultivation of moral virtue may be simply too difficult to avoid due to the inherent inability to effectively regulate access to various forms of enhancement once they become marketable.[280]

Eberl argues that at least one should have a second-level order of desiring improving in one's own virtuous life and freely choosing to enhance it, as long as this choosing is always directed towards human flourishing and it is a real improvement.

6.3 Miracles and the Laws of Nature

Another important topic in which Thomists have engaged with philosophy of science is the case of the possibility of miracles in relation to the ontological status of the laws of nature. Interestingly, a vast number of Neo-Thomist authors framed their discussion about the possibility of miracles around the idea of the laws of nature, a notion alien to Thomas Aquinas himself. In fact, Aquinas brought a rather different metaphysical tool for asserting that miracles were possible, namely, obediential potency.[281] Still, by the early twentieth century, the notion of the laws of nature was so engraved in the view of nature, and, not least importantly, was used to deny the very possibility of miracles by the followers of Hume, that Thomist scholars faced the challenge of addressing this issue, and many discussed the possibility of miracles in direct reference to the modern notion of the laws of nature within the treatises of natural philosophy. Authors like Juan José Urráburu,[282] Joseph Gredt,[283] Édouard Hugon,[284] and even the great

---

[278] Eberl 2014, 301.   [279] Eberl 2018, 514.   [280] Eberl 2014, 306.   [281] Silva 2024b.
[282] Urráburu 1892, 361–449.   [283] Gredt 1937, 275–281.   [284] Hugon 1905, 277–298.

Réginald Garrigou-Lagrange,[285] among many others, all make use of this modern notion in their Thomistic theology.

The main trend among them is to interpret the laws of nature as being real laws ordained by God to nature having a conditional or hypothetical necessity. This type of necessity, the key to solving the issue of miracles, is explained both in terms of the natural conditions surrounding an event and in terms of the divine concurrence to every action in nature as primary cause. Thus, the argument holds that a miracle occurs when God withdraws (or reinforces) this divine concurrence in the action of secondary causes. Simply put, since the laws of nature work under the condition of God's concurrent causation with secondary causes, were God to change this causation, the laws of nature would be momentarily suspended. Closer to us today, Vincent Guagliardo, OP, and Michael Dodds, OP, also discuss miracles framed within the notion of the laws of nature suggesting, as well, that God could reinforce and withdraw his own concursus with secondary causes.[286]

6.4 The Origin of Life

In direct relation with the possibility of miracles is that of the origin of life, a question that keeps many a scientist awake even today. Regardless of what the best definition of life is, how it originated remains one of the most intriguing enterprises into which the most diverse scientific disciplines have some input. Thomists, as can be expected, have also tackled this evasive question with diverse strategies. Thomas Aquinas left many doors open to his followers on this matter. He claimed, for instance, when commenting on the six days of creation, that plants appeared through the active action of the heavenly bodies and the passive reception of the earth: '[for] the production of plants from the earth into actual existence ... the powers of the heavenly body as father, and of the earth as mother suffice'.[287] As well, there are some small living beings that are produced by putrefaction without the intervention of previous living beings: 'For these the power of celestial bodies along with appropriate matter is sufficient.'[288] Moreover, when discussing the doctrine of creation, he clearly states that although being is through creation, 'life and others of the like are by information', that is, by the action of secondary causes.[289]

---

[285] Garrigou-Lagrange 1950, 330–336.
[286] Guagliardo 1990, 17–20; Dodds 2012, 252–257. Other thinkers within the Thomist tradition have also discussed the notion of the laws of nature, for instance, Stoeger 2001, who argues that laws of nature are descriptive and not prescriptive, though he does not refer explicitly to their relation to miracles within a Thomistic framework.
[287] *De Pot.* 4, 2, ad 28.   [288] *Super II Sent.*, 1, 1, 4, co.   [289] *De Pot.*, q. 3, a. 1, co.

Still, there is an almost unanimous voice among Thomists, at least since the early twentieth century, that the first living being was directly created by God at some point in the early Earth. Mercier, for instance, has claimed that 'in the presence of the manifestly temporary duration of organised substances the necessity of an extrinsic cause from which life proceeds is obvious'.[290] Calling on Pasteur's demonstrations that denied the existence of spontaneous generation, Mercier affirmed that 'it was originally required a direct intervention from the Author of nature for the production of the first living beings'.[291] In the same line, Gredt also affirmed the necessity of God's intervention: 'the first origin of corporeal life cannot be explained except by the intervention of a first cause, which created living bodies out of nothing, or rather formed them from matter already existing'.[292]

Contemporary Thomists have also discussed this question, mostly following the same idea that God is required to create directly the first living being. For instance, William Carroll has expressed that

> 'if inanimate things were in themselves to possess the power to cause living things to come into existence, in some way, then it seems that they, these inanimate things, would not be inanimate but rather living things themselves ... If inanimate things by nature could cause living things to emerge, God would be creating that which was and that which was not what it is ... So, it seems to me that the initial emergence of life requires something more than natural causes functioning in the ordinary way according to which nature and God are the complete causes of what happens in the world.[293]

Mariusz Tabaczek, however, has hinted at a model to explain the possibility of life emerging from the regular actions of non-living natural causes. Appealing to the *dynamic* moments of God's action in nature, in particular, the idea that natural causes act as instruments of the primary causality of God, Tabaczek explains that

> this model of divine action makes plausible a suggestion that life emerged spontaneously, as an outcome of natural causes, which nonetheless operated as secondary and instrumental factors moved by God who is the primary and principal cause of all changes in the created universe. In other words, the origin of life would be an outcome of a concurrence of divine (transcendent) and created (immanent) action.[294]

Interestingly, writing with Chilean biochemist Rafael Vicuña, William Carroll had suggested something similar to this position as well a few years before (even if he expressed a different view when writing alone later on): 'if we were

---

[290] Mercier 1887–88, 53. [291] Mercier 1887–88, 54. [292] Gredt 1937, 490.
[293] Carroll 2022. [294] Tabaczek 2023a, 13.

to discover that life itself in its very beginnings can emerge from natural causes, it does not mean that God is not the origin of living things. It means that causal potentialities in nature are robust enough that a living thing can be the result of processes that begin with non-living matter'.[295]

6.5 Ecology

Ecology has of late been another topic which has offered a fertile ground for Thomists. Called by Pope Francis' encyclical *Laudato Si'*, American philosopher and theologian Christopher Thompson invites Thomist scholars to consider what he has termed Green Thomism, that is, 'the retrieval of St. Thomas' vision of creation and the unique vocation of human beings within it, in order to inspire a more robust spiritual life with integral ecology at its core'.[296] In a clear invitation similar to what I have called science-engaged Thomism, Thompson argues that 'Thomists could profit from the engagement of modern cultural movements such as the rise of environmental concern'.[297] For him, since 'the philosophical framework supplied by St. Thomas regarding "the nature of nature" and the vision of the human person as a union of both material and spiritual principles can provide the necessary components of an integral ecology'.[298] The human person is, thus, at the very core of Green Thomism, which affirms that, even after original sin, 'the wisdom of the Creator still permeates creation and provides norms for its care as well as human flourishing'.[299] This natural world is, metaphysically and theologically speaking, the world of Thomas Aquinas, and, thus, is conceived as an 'order utterly dependent upon a provident First Cause, whose causality extends to the operations of individual creatures'.[300] As such, it can renew an eco-realism by supplying a rich notion of the person as the subject who stewards created things that need to be stewarded. Thus, Green Thomism is properly manifested 'in imitating the divine posture before creation: the receptive contemplation of the goodness of things', which is nothing more than the stewardship over creation as the human participation in the eternal law, that is, natural law.[301] It is, then, the natural law tradition that can 'affirm not only the dignity and value of the various creatures and our relationship to them, but outline more completely how human beings are to treat the environment'.[302]

Thompson's ideas are complemented by two further developments within Thomism in relation to ecology. First, that of Judith Barad, who in the final decades of the last century proposed a reinterpretation of Aquinas' hierarchy of

---

[295] Carroll and Vicuña 2017, 38.   [296] Thompson 2017, 9.   [297] Thompson 2017, 9.
[298] Thompson 2017, 10.   [299] Thompson 2017, 23.   [300] Thompson 2017, 27.
[301] Thompson 2017, 43.   [302] Thompson 2017, 45.

material beings, that is, from inanimate things, through plants and animals, to human beings to suggest that higher animals might also be subjects of rights coming out of natural law. The idea is the following. Since, according to Aquinas, 'the lowest species of animals are continuous with the highest forms of plants and the highest forms of animals are continuous with the lowest forms of human nature',[303] it comes as no surprise that higher animals are conceived as sentient beings, capable of some kind of rudimentary understanding and volition. Thus, Barad affirms that, if one follows Aquinas, one should conclude that 'animals have a rich affective life, complete with emotions and desires'.[304] Now, these emotions and desires, as well as their capacity for different kinds of knowledge (albeit not intellectual), proceed from the very nature of animals, and, as such, are a tendency towards their own good. Hence, Barad concludes, 'since human beings and animals have inclinations to pursue goods completing their natures, and since human beings are granted rights based on their natural inclinations, perhaps animals capable of apprehension should also be granted rights on the basis of their natural inclinations'.[305] In a way, Barad argues, 'animals participate in the same eternal law as human beings'.[306]

This language of participation is what Andrew Davison makes use of to move forward the conversation between Thomism and ecology, since this metaphysical notion of participation is the very root of the real value of all natural things. In fact, Davison finds that the 'association of participation in God with notions of gift offers ready parallels to a participatory account of environmental responsibility, and of human embeddedness in nature',[307] opening thus the possibility of a fruitful engagement between participatory theology and ecology. Given that every creature participates in God's being, 'each creature would stand before us as a being in which something of God is expressed'.[308] In this sense, within a theology of participation 'each thing will thrive according to its nature, according to its particular mode of participation in God'.[309] Davison, thus, concludes, that 'if each creature, and each kind of creature, is celebrated as a particular finite participation in divine plenitude, then those creaturely natures, and their modes of activity, take on a sacred quality'.[310]

Davison draws, however, another kind of participation from Aquinas' teachings, namely, categorical participation, to account for the interrelations present in nature of which ecology speaks today. This categorical participation refers to the fact that each member of a species is, at the same part, a member of a larger group, traditionally referred to as genus. Thus, for instance, a lion shares with other lions in their being lions, but also shares with panthers and cheetahs being

---

[303] Barad 1988, 103. [304] Barad 1988, 107. [305] Barad 1988, 109. [306] Barad 1988, 109.
[307] Davison 2022, 83. [308] Davison 2022, 85. [309] Davison 2022, 87.
[310] Davison 2022, 87.

part of the genus of cats. Similarly, human beings participate in being animals with other sentient beings. This predicamental participation makes direct reference to the order of the world and the interrelations between species existing within that order.

Finally, considering the Thomistic doctrine of participation, both theological and predicamental, Davison affirms the relative, though significant, value of created reality, which ultimately depends on God for its being, but that, given God's infinite goodness, as Aquinas taught, possesses the dignity of being and acting according to that being. Thus, Davison affirms both, that 'attention to nature need not displace God'[311] and that 'on a participatory view, creation is neither ultimate nor degraded. It comes from God and has its value from God'.[312]

6.6 Embryology

I will finish this quick review of contemporary Thomistic engagements with the sciences with one theological example of science-engaged Thomism that specifically considers developmental embryology, particularly on the role of Mary in the Incarnation. Following on a similar strategy than that of Aquinas when considering this issue, Juan Eduardo Carreño, a Chilean medical doctor and philosopher, has strongly argued that 'modern biological data offers room to underline further the *active* role of the Mother of God in the generation of her Son',[313] directly engaging in his interpretation of this doctrine with embryological science. For Carreño, 'it seems reasonable to speculate that the *immediate* corporal disposition the Virgin could have offered with her acceptance consisted of an oocyte capable of fertilization', which 'has a series of peculiarities that distinguish it from other cells, including a haploid set of chromosomes, abundant cytoplasmic organelles, and a still partially known series of cytosolic, nuclear, and membrane elements and factors that make it suitable to generate, under the right conditions, a new organism of the human species'.[314] Carreño emphasises that this oocyte is the immediate disposition, but that one cannot neglect considering the whole of Mary's body, since 'the sexual cell the Virgin presumably provides for the conception of Jesus Christ is the corollary of a chain of physiological processes that, ultimately, involve the whole of her bodily economy'.[315] In this sense, Mary put her entire body in God's hands, and not only the oocyte, as, for instance, Aquinas' own interpretations of the dogma had considered previously. Thus, Carreño moves forward the Thomistic traditional interpretation, suggesting, with contemporary embryology, that a woman

---
[311] Davison 2022, 93. [312] Davison 2022, 94. [313] Carreño 2024a, 82 (my emphasis).
[314] Carreño 2024a, 92. [315] Carreño 2024a, 92.

is involved genetically and molecularly, biochemically, physiologically, and morphologically in the gestation of the child, showing an active role in this generation and gestation.[316] In fact, Carreño strongly suggests that understanding the role of Mary in the Incarnation allows the theologian to recognise that this event happened at the same instant that Jesus was conceived, being able, thus, to reject certain erroneous interpretations of the doctrine, such as that of adoptionism that would claim that the Second Person adopted an already conceived human being. Offering a quite detailed description of the biological process that the human zygote undergoes from conception until birth, Carreño affirms that it 'reveals a chain of events that connect one to another in a fundamentally continuous sequence, from the conception of the zygote until the death of the individual',[317] suggesting, given that it is the Second Person who assumed human nature in full, including all the morphogenetic process, that 'it is coherent – although not absolutely necessary – the Incarnation coincides with the only milestone that involves a substantial change, namely, conception'.[318] For Carreño, even if biology cannot modify what the magisterium defined, 'a critical and cautious assimilation of facts described by particular sciences can illuminate aspects of dogma that would otherwise remain unspoken or only partially outlined',[319] as in the case of the causal role of the Virgin Mary in the conception of her Son.

7 Conclusion

Thomism has engaged throughout its history with the knowledge of the natural world. In the end, as a realist philosophy, Thomism is committed to knowing reality and from this knowledge arises to the knowledge of its Creator. I have offered in this Element a new label, science-engaged Thomism, for a strategy on how to perform this task. I have argued that this new strategy is already present in the works of many a Thomist today and in the recent past, and I have compared it to some older strategies present in the works of some Neo-Thomists. Andrew Davison has of late articulated this idea in rather telling terms: 'Thomism, seeking to be neither defensive nor revisionary, and valuing both openness and confidence, offers a form of theology that is both appealing on its own terms, and particularly open to conversations about scientific topics.'[320] I have attempted to show how Thomism is constantly developing by engaging with the problems and debates of each era.

Of course, this new Thomist perspective by no means neglects the fact that Thomism has engaged in different ways with the sciences in its enormous

---

[316] Carreño 2024a, 97.   [317] Carreño 2024a, 96.   [318] Carreño 2024a, 97.
[319] Carreño 2024a, 100.   [320] Davison 2023, 15.

tradition, as it has become clear throughout these pages. My understanding of science-engaged Thomism is that it is a way of approaching the sciences to answer specific questions within Thomism, both philosophical and theological questions appealing to scientific knowledge. In addition, my portrayal of science-engaged Thomism allows for specific as well as general questions. Finally, science-engaged Thomism as described in this Element embraces any kind of engagement with the sciences, both (1) to respond precise questions, as in the case of the role of Mary in the Incarnation of the Second Person of the Trinity in Jesus Christ; and (2) to allow some particular science to inspire and influence new metaphysical or theological doctrinal developments, as in the cases of the doctrine of divine providence and natural indeterminism, the case of the origins of the cosmos and the doctrine of creation, or even the doctrine of the Incarnation in light of astrobiology.

Thomism, thus, can gain much from its interaction with contemporary sciences. Particularly, my suggestion is that when Thomists 'make claims about created, empirical realities, they should incorporate the insights of empirical investigation into their analysis', as Perry and Leidenhag suggest for any theologian.[321] This means that the Thomist would not consider Thomism as a closed philosophical and theological system, but rather approach the thought and teachings of Thomas Aquinas as a metaphysical and theological toolbox, which, paired with the findings of the contemporary sciences, can be used to solve and develop certain philosophical and theological questions and doctrines. Ultimately, this is a call for a humble approach to reality and to how we know reality in the search for an advance in our knowledge of the divine and its creation, always guided by the wisdom of Thomas Aquinas.

---

[321] Perry and Leidenhag 2023, 64.

Abbreviations of Thomas Aquinas' Works

Aquinas' works are taken from Enrique Alarcón, ed., *Corpus Thomisticum*. Pamplona: Universitatis Studiorum Navarrensis. 2000. www.corpusthomisticum.org.

De Ente et Essentia (1252/56)	*De Ente*
Expositio super librum De Causis (1271–72)	*In De Causis*
Quaestiones Disputatae De Malo (1266–67)	*De Malo*
Quaestiones Disputatae De Potentia Dei (1265–66)	*De Pot.*
Scriptum super libros Sententiarum (1251–56)	*In Sent.*
Sententia libri Metaphysicae (1269–72)	*In Met.*
Sententia libri De Anima (1269–70)	*In De An.*
Summa Contra Gentiles (1259–64)	*SCG*
Summa Theologiae (1266–73)	*S.Th.*

References

Asla, Mariano (2019). On the Limits, Imperfections and Evils of the Human Condition: Biological Improvement from a Thomistic Perspective. *Scientia et Fides*, 7(2): 77–95.

Aubert, Jean-Marie (1965). *Philosophie de la Nature*. Paris: Beauchesne.

Austriaco, Nicanor (2003). In Defense of Double Agency in Evolution: A Response to Five Modern Critics. *Angelicum*, 80(4): 947–966.

Austriaco, Nicanor (2015). A Theological Fittingness Argument for the Historicity of the Fall of *Homo Sapiens*. *Nova et Vetera*, 13(3): 651–668.

Austriaco, Nicanor (2017). In Defense of Thomistic Evolution: A Response to Chaberek. *Public Discourse*, 07 March. www.thepublicdiscourse.com/2018/03/20975/.

Austriaco, Nicanor, Baptist Ku, Thomas Davenport, James Brent, et al. (2020). *Thomistic Evolution*. Providence, RI: Clunny Media.

Barad, Judith (1988). Aquinas' Inconsistency on the Nature and the Treatment of Animals. *Between the Species*, 4(2): 102–111.

Beltrán, Oscar H. (2009). Teología y ciencia en la obra de Santo Tomás de Aquino. *Revista Teología*, 46: 281–299.

Boedder, Bernard (1891). *Natural Theology*. New York: Longmans, Green.

Boulding, Jamie (2022). *The Multiverse and Participatory Metaphysics*. Abingdon: Routledge.

Brooke, John H. (1991). *Science and Religion: Some Historical Perspectives*. Cambridge: Cambridge University Press.

Cantin, Stanislas (1948). *Précis de psychologie thomiste*. Québec: Les Presses de l'Université Laval.

Carreño, Juan Eduardo (2024a). Theology, Philosophy, and Biology: An Interpretation of the Conception of Jesus Christ. *Nova et Vetera*, 22(1): 71–102.

Carreño, Juan Eduardo (2024b). *Thomistic Philosophy in the Face of Evolutionary Fact*. Neunkirchen-Seelscheid: editiones-scholasticae.

Carroll, William E. (2000). Creation, Evolution, and Thomas Aquinas. *Revue des Questions Scientifiques*, 171(4): 319–347.

Carroll, William E. (2008). Divine Agency, Contemporary Physics, and the Autonomy of Nature. *The Heytrop Journal*, 49: 582–602.

Carroll, William E. (2010). Creation and the Foundations of Evolution. *Angelicum*, 87: 45–60.

Carroll, William E. (2012). Cosmology and Creation: From Hawking to Aquinas. *Logos: A Journal of Catholic Thought and Culture*, 15(1): 134–149.

Carroll, William E. (2022). *Causes and the Origin of Life: Philosophy of Nature, Metaphysics, and Theology* (Video) – Thomistic Institute, 1 April. https://angelicum.it/thomistic-institute/it/2022/04/01/causes-and-the-origin-of-life-video/ (accessed on 2 May 2024).

Carroll, William E. and Rafael Vicuña (2017). God, Nature and the Origin of Life. *Science & Christian Belief*, 29: 37–41.

Cessario, Romanus (2003). *A Short History of Thomism*. Washington, DC: The Catholic University of America Press.

Chaberek, Michael (2017). *Aquinas and Evolution*. Leicester: The Chartwell Press.

Cipolla, Richard G. (1974). Selvaggi Revisited: Transubstantiation and Contemporary Science. *Theological Studies*, 35(4): 667–691.

Clark, Joseph T. (1951). Physics, Philosophy, Transubstantiation, Theology. *Theological Studies*, 12: 24–25.

Clayton, Philip (2004). Natural Law and Divine Action: The Search for an Expanded Theory of Causation. *Zygon*, 39(3): 615–636.

Collin, Henri (1926). *Manuel de Philosophie Thomiste*. Paris: Pierre Téqui éditeur.

Colombo, Carlo (1955). Teologia, filosofia, e fisica nella dottrina della transustanziazione. *Scuola Cattolica*, 83: 89–124.

Colombo, Carlo (1956). Ancora sulla dottrina della transustanziazione e la fisica moderna. *Scuola Cattolica*, 84: 263–288.

Colombo, Carlo (1960). Bilancio provvisorio di una discussione eucaristica. *Scuola Cattolica*, 88: 23–55.

Coppens, Charles (1891). *A Brief Text-Book of Logic and Mental Philosophy*. New York: Schwartz, Kirwin & Fauss.

Davison, Andrew (2018a). 'He Fathers-Forth Whose Beauty Is Past Change', but 'Who Knows How?': Evolution and Divine Exemplarity. *Nova et Vetera*, 16(4): 1067–1102.

Davison, Andrew (2018b). Looking Back toward the Origin: Scientific Cosmology as Creation ex nihilo Considered 'from the Inside'. Gary Anderson and Markus Bockmuehl, eds., *Creatio ex nihilo: Origins, Development, Contemporary Challenges*. Notre Dame: Notre Dame University Press, 367–389.

Davison, Andrew (2022). Participation and Nature in Christian Theology. Alexander J. B. Hampton and Douglas Hedley, eds., *The Cambridge Companion to Christianity and the Environment*. Cambridge: Cambridge University Press, 80–95.

Davison, Andrew (2023). *Astrobiology and Christian Doctrine: Exploring the Implications of Life in the Universe*. Cambridge: Cambridge University Press.

de Haan, Daniel (2017). Hylomorphic Animalism, Emergentism, and the Challenge of the New Mechanist Philosophy of Neuroscience. *Scientia et Fides*, 5(2): 9–38.

de Haan, Daniel (2018). The Interaction of Noetic and Psychosomatic Operations in a Thomist Hylomorphic Anthropology. *Scientia et Fides*, 6(2): 55–83.

de Koninck, Charles (1937). Réflexions sur le problème de l'indéterminisme. *Revue Thomiste*, 43(2–3): 227–252 and 393–409.

de Koninck, Charles (1961). Darwin's Dilemma. *The Thomist: A Speculative Quarterly Review*, 24(2): 367–382.

de Koninck, Charles (2008). The Cosmos: Charles de Koninck. Ralph McInerny, ed. *The Writings of Charles de Koninck*, trans. Ralph McInerny. Notre Dame: Notre Dame Press.

Deely, John (1973). *The Problem of Evolution: A Study of the Philosophical Repercussions of Evolutionary Science*. New York: Appleton-Century-Croft.

Dodds, Michael (2012). *Unlocking Divine Action*. Washington, DC: The Catholic University of America Press.

Donat, Josef (1934). *Summa Philosophiae Christianae*. Innsbruck: Felicianus Rauch.

Dorlodot, Henry de (1921). *Le Darwinisme au Point de Vue de l'Orthodoxie Catholique*. Bruxelles, Paris: Vromant.

Dorlodot, Henry de (1922). *Darwinism and Catholic Thought*. New York: Burns, Oates and Washbourne.

Dorlodot, Henry de (2009). *L'Origine de l'homme: Le Darwinisme au Point de Vue de l'Orthodoxie Catholique*. Wavre: Mardaga.

Doronzo, Emmanuel (1968). *Theologia Dogmatica. Vol. II*. Washington, DC: The Catholic University of America.

Eberl, Jason (2014). A Thomistic Appraisal of Human Enhancement Technologies. *Theoretical Medicine and Bioethics*, 35(4): 289–310.

Eberl, Jason (2018). Can Prudence Be Enhanced? *The Journal of Medicine and Philosophy: A Forum for Bioethics and Philosophy of Medicine*, 43(5): 506–526.

Eberl, Jason (2022). Enhancing the Imago Dei: Can a Christian Be a Transhumanist? *Christian Bioethics: Non-Ecumenical Studies in Medical Morality*, 28(1): 76–93.

Elders, Leo (1997). Modern Science and the Philosophy of Nature. Mario Enrique Sacchi, ed., *Ministerium Verbi: Estudios dedicados* a Monseñor Héctor Aguer en ocasión del XXV aniversario de su ordenación sacerdotal. Buenos Aires: Basileia, 111–122.

Elders, Leo (2020). Joseph Gredt, O.S.B., *Elementa philosophiae aristotelico-thomisticae*. 1899–1901. Serge-Thomas Bonino, ed., *Grandi opere del Tomismo nel Novecento*. Rome: Urbaniana University Press, 13–26.

Fabro, Cornelio (2022). *Introduction to St. Thomas: Thomistic Metaphysics and Modern Thought*. Chillum, MD: IVE Press.

Farges, Albert and Désiré Barbedette (1921). *Philosophia scholastica ad mentem S. Thomae Aquinatis exposita et recentioribus scientiarum inventis aptata, 31st ed*. Parisiis: Apud Baston, Berche et Pagis.

Feser, Edward (2019). *Aristotle's Revenge: The Metaphysical Foundations of Physical and Biological Science*. Neunkirchen-Seelscheid: editiones-scholasticae.

Flipse, Abraham C. (2008). Between Neo-Thomist Natural Philosophy and Secular Science: Roman Catholic Scientists in the Netherlands, 1900–1950. *Styles of Thinking in Science and Technology. Proceeding of the Third International Conference of the European Society for the History of Science 2008*, 1146–1151.

Frank, Karl (1913). *The Theory of Evolution in Light of Facts*. London: Kegan Paul, Trench, Trubner.

Frank, Karl (1926). *Cursus Philosophicus in Usum Scholarum: Philosophia Naturalis*. Friburgi: Herder.

Gardeil, Ambroise (1893). L'Evolutionism et les Principes de S. Thomas. *Revue Thomiste*, 1(1): 27–45.

Gardeil, Ambroise (1894). L'Evolutionism et les Principes de S. Thomas – II – Les Systèmes. *Revue Thomiste*, 2(1): 29–42.

Gardeil, Ambroise (1895). L'Evolutionism et les Principes de S. Thomas – II – Les Systèmes (*cont.*). *Revue Thomiste*, 3(1): 61–84.

Gardeil, Ambroise (1896). L'Evolutionism et les Principes de S. Thomas – III – Conciliation. *Revue Thomiste*, 4(1): 215–247.

Gardeil, Henri Dominique (1966). *Initiation a la Philosophie de Saint Thomas d'Aquin*. Paris: Les Éditions du Cerf.

Garrigou-Lagrange, Réginald (1950). *De Revelatione II*. Paris: Lethielleux.

Gilson, Étienne (2009). *From Aristotle to Darwin and Back Again: A Journey in Final Causality, Species and Evolution*. San Francisco, CA: Ignatius Press.

González Arintero, Juan (1898). *La Evolución y la Filosofía Cristina*. Madrid: Librería de Gregorio del Amo.

González y Díaz Tuñón, Zeferino (1864). *Estudios sobre la Filosofía de Santo Tomás*. Tomo II. Manila: Establecimiento Tipográfico del Colegio de Santo Tomás.

González y Díaz Tuñón, Zeferino (1873). *Filosofía Elemental*. Madrid: Policarpo López.

González y Díaz Tuñón, Zeferino (1886). *Historia de la Filosofía*. Madrid: A. Jubera.

González y Díaz Tuñón, Zeferino (1891). *La Biblia y la Ciencia*. Madrid: Imprenta de A. Pérez Dubrull.

Gredt, Josephus (1899). *Elementa Philosophiae Aristotelico-Thomisticae, vol. I, 1st ed.* Rome: Descleé.

Gredt, Josephus (1937). *Elementa Philosophiae Aristotelico-Thomisticae, vol. II, 7th ed.* Barcelona: Herder.

Gredt, Josephus (1946). *Elementa Philosophiae Aristotelico-Thomisticae, vol. I, 8th ed.* Barcelona: Herder.

Grenier, Henri (1944). *Cursus philosophiae: volumen primum continens introductionem generalem, logicam et philosophiam naturalem*. Quebeci: Le Seminaire de Quebec.

Guagliardo, Vincent (1990). Nature and Miracle. *CTNS Bulletin*, 10(2): 17–20.

Harrison, Peter (2021). A Historian's Perspective on Science-Engaged Theology. *Modern Theology*, 37(2): 476–482.

Hayward Joyce, George (1922). *Principles of Natural Theology*. New York: Longmans, Green.

Heisenberg, Werner (1927). Über den anschaulichen Inhalt der quantentheoretischen Kinematik und Mechanik. *Zeitschrift für Physik*, 43: 172–198.

Heisenberg, Werner (1958). *Physics and Philosophy*. New York: Prometheus Books.

Hellín, Iosephus (1950). *Cursus Philosophicus: Theologia Naturalis*. Madrid: BAC.

Hoenen, Petrus (1956). *Cosmologia*. Romae: Apud Aedes Universitates Gregorianae.

Houck, Daniel W. (2020). *Aquinas, Original Sin, and the Challenge of Evolution*. Cambridge: Cambridge University Press.

Hudson, Deal W. (1992). The Future of Thomism: An Introduction. Deal W. Hudson and Dennis Moran, eds., *The Future of Thomism*. Mishawaka, IN: American Maritain Association, 7–21.

Hugon, Édouard (1905). *Cursus Philosophiae Thomisticae, II Philosophia Naturalis: Cosmologia*. Paris: Lethielleux.

Jolivet, Régis (1940). *Traité de philosophie: Psychologie*. Lyon: Emmanuel Vitte.

Keltz, Kyle (2020). *Thoand the Problem of Animal Suffering*. Eugene, OR: Wipf & Stock.

References

Kennedy, Leonard (1987). *A Catalogue of Thomists, 1270–1900*. Houston, TX: Center for Thomistic Studies, University of St. Thomas.

Kittle, Simon (2022). God Is (Probably) a Cause among Causes: Why the Primary/Secondary Cause Distinction Doesn't Help in Developing Non-Interventionist Accounts of Special Divine Action. *Theology and Science*, 20(2): 247–262.

Koons, Robert (2022). *Is St. Thomas's Aristotelian Philosophy of Nature Obsolete?* South Bend, IN: St. Augustine Press.

Kopf, Simon (2022). *Reframing Providence: New Perspectives from Aquinas on the Divine Action Debate*. Oxford: Oxford University Press.

Kopf, Simon (2023). *Reframing Providence. New Perspectives from Aquinas on the Divine Action Debate*. Oxford: Oxford University Press.

Kopf, Simon (2024). Science-Engaged Thomism. *Religions*, 15(5): 1–22, 591.

Koren, Henry (1955). *An Introduction to the Philosophy of Animate Nature*. St. Louis, MO: B. Herder Book.

Lazzari, Edmund (2025). The Divine Nature Is Not a Cause among Causes: A Response to Kittle and Sollereder. *Theology and Science*, 543–555.

Lemaître, Georges (1931). The Beginning of the World from the Point of View of Quantum Theory. *Nature*, 127: 706.

Lortie, Stanislas-Alfred (1917). *Elementa philosophiae christianae ad mentem s. Thomae Aquinatis exposita, 3rd ed.* Quebeci: L'Action sociale.

Maria, Michaele de (1913). *Philosophia peripatetico-scholastica ex fontibus Aristotelis et S. Thomae Aquinatis expressa et ad adolescentium institutionem accommodata, vol. 2, 4th ed.* Romae: ex Pontificia Officina Typographica.

Maritain, Jacques (1959). *Distinguish to Unite: Or the Degrees of Knowledge*. New York: Charles Scribner's Sons.

Maritain, Jacques (1967). Vers une idée thomiste de l'évolution. *Nova et Vetera*, 42: 130–131.

Masi, Roberto (1955). Teologia eucaristica e fisica contemporanea. *Doctor Communis*, 8: 31–51.

Masi, Roberto (1957). La sostanza materiale ed i suoi accidenti – La conversione eucaristica. *Studia Patavina*, 4.

Melsen, A. G. M. van (1965). *Evolution and Philosophy*. Pittsburgh, PA: Duquesne University Press.

Mercier, Désiré (1887–88). *Cours de Philosophie selon S. Thomas d'Aquin: La Psychologie*. Autographie de Charles Peeters: Louvain.

Mivart, St. George Jackson (1871). *On the Genesis of Species*. London & New York: MacMillan.

Munier, André (1956). *Manuel de philosophie, vol. 1*. Paris: Desclée.

Nogar, Raymond (1963). *The Wisdom of Evolution*. New York: Doubleday.

Pawl, Timothy (2016). Thomistic Multiple Incarnations. *The Heythrop Journal*, 57: 359–370.

Pègues, Thomas (1927). *Aperçus de philosophie thomiste et de propédeutique*. Paris: André Blot Editeur.

Perry, John and Joanna Leidenhag (2021). What Is Science-Engaged Theology. *Modern Theology*, 37(2): 245–253.

Perry, John and Joanna Leidenhag (2023). *Science-Engaged Theology*. Cambridge: Cambridge University Press.

Pesch, Tilmann (1880). *Institutiones philosophiae naturalis secundum principia S. Thomae Aquinatis, ad usum scholasticum accommodavit*. Friburgi: sumptibus Herder.

Pesch, Tilmannus (1897). *Institutiones Philosophiae Naturalis secundum Principia S. Thomae Aquinatis, ad usum scholsticum accommodavit, vol. II*. Friburg: Herder.

Phillips, Richard Percival (1964). *Modern Thomistic Philosophy*. Westminster: The Newman Press.

Pirotta, Angelo (1936). *Summa Philosophiae Aristotelico-Thomisticae, vol. 2: Philosophia Naturalis Generalis et Specialis*. Taurini: Mariett.

Pohle, Joseph (1917). *God, the Author of Nature and the Supernatural (De Deo Creante et Elevante). A Dogmatic Treatise*. St. Louis, MO & London: B. Herder.

Polkinghorne, John (1995). The Metaphysics of Divine Action. Robert Russell, Nancy Murphy, and Arthur Peacocke, eds., *Chaos and Complexity. Scientific Perspectives on Divine Action*. Vatican City – Berkeley, CA: Vatican Observatory – CTNS, 147–156.

Polkinghorne, John (2000). *Faith, Science, and Understanding*. New Haven, CT-London: Yale University Press.

Pope Leo XIII (1879). *Aeterni Patris. Encyclical on the Restoration of Christian Philosophy*. www.vatican.va/content/leo-xiii/en/encyclicals/documents/hf_l-xiii_enc_04081879_aeterni-patris.html.

Rahner, Karl (1983). *On Recognising the Importance of Thomas Aquinas: Theological Investigations XIII*. New York: Crossroad Books.

Reese, Philip-Neri (2024). Losing the Forest for the Tree: Why All Thomists Should (Not) Be River Forest Thomists. *Religions*, 15(5): 1–17, 569.

Russell, Robert John (2006). Quantum Physics and the Theology of Non-Interventionist Objective Divine Action. Philip Clayton, ed., *The Oxford Handbook of Religion and Science*. Oxford: Oxford University Press, 579–595.

Salcedo, Leovigildo (1952). *Philosophiae Scholasticae Summa*. Madrid: BAC.

Sanguineti, Juan José (2023). God in the Face of Natural and Moral Evils: A Thomistic Approach. *Religions*, 14(7): 1–26, 816.

Selvaggi, Filippo (1949). Il concetto di sostanza nel Dogma Eucaristico in relazione alla fisica moderna. *Gregorianum*, 30(1/2): 7–45.

Selvaggi, Filippo (1956). Realtà fisica e sostanza sensibile nella dottrina eucaristica. *Gregorianum*, 37: 16–33.

Selvaggi, Filippo (1957). Ancora interno ai concetti di 'sostanza sensibile' e 'realtà fisica'. *Gregorianum*, 38: 503–514.

Selvaggi, Filippo (1959). *Cosmologia*. Romae: Apud Aedes Universitates Gregorianae.

Selvaggi, Filippo (1962). *Scienza e Metodologia*. Roma: Editrice Università Gregoriana.

Selvaggi, Filippo (1964). *Causalità e indeterminismo: La problematica moderna alla luce della filosofia aristotelico-tomista*. Roma: Editrice Università Gregoriana.

Sertillanges, Antonin (1945). *L'Idée de Création et ses Retentissements en Philosophie*. Paris: Éditions Montaigne.

Silva, Ignacio (2013). Thomas Aquinas Holds Fast: Objections to Aquinas within Today's Debate on Divine Action. *The Heythrop Journal*, 54(4): 658–667.

Silva, Ignacio (2014). Revisiting Aquinas on Providence and Rising to the Challenge of Divine Action in Nature. *The Journal of Religion*, 94(3): 277–291.

Silva, Ignacio (2015). Providence, Contingency, and the Perfection of the Cosmos. *Philosophy, Theology and the Sciences*, 2(2): 137–157.

Silva, Ignacio (2022). *Providence and Science in a World of Contingency*. Abingdon: Routledge.

Silva, Ignacio (2024a). Neo-Thomism on Evolution. Erkki V. R. Kojonen and Shuaib Ahmed Malik, eds., *Design Discourse in Abrahamic Traditions: History, Metaphysics, and Science*. Abingdon: Routledge. 110–128.

Silva, Ignacio (2024b). Thomas Aquinas and Some Neo-Thomists on the Possibility of Miracles and the Laws of Nature. *Religions*, 15(4): 422, 1–14.

Silva, Ignacio and Gonzalo Recio (2023). Aquinas' Science-Engaged Theology. *Religious Studies*, 61(1), 179–193.

Simpson, William. M. R. (2022). From Quantum Physics to Classical Metaphysics. William M. R. Simpson, Robert C. Koons, and James Orr, eds., *Neo-Aristotelian Metaphysics and the Theology of Nature*. New York: Routledge, 21–65.

Sollereder, Bethany (2015). A Modest Objection: Neo-Thomism and God as a Cause among Causes. *Theology and Science*, 13(3): 345–353.

Stoeger, William (1995). Describing God's Action in the World in Light of Scientific Knowledge of Reality. Robert Russell, Nancy Murphy, and Arthur Peacocke, eds., *Chaos and Complexity: Scientific Perspectives on Divine Action*. Vatican City – Berkeley, CA: Vatican Observatory – CTNS, 239–261.

Stoeger, William R. (2001). Contemporary Physics and the Ontological Status of the Laws of Nature. Robert Russell, Nancy Murphy, and Christopher J. Isham, eds., *Quantum Cosmology and the Laws of Nature: Scientific Perspectives on Divine Action*. Vatican City – Berkeley, CA: Vatican Observatory – CTNS, 207–231.

Tabaczek, Mariusz (2022). Does God Create through Evolution? A Thomistic Perspective. *Theology and Science*, 20(1): 46–68.

Tabaczek, Mariusz (2023a). Aristotelian-Thomistic Contribution to the Contemporary Studies on Biological Life and Its Origin. *Religions*, 14(2): 1–25, 214.

Tabaczek, Mariusz (2023b). Human Enhancement, Transhumanism, and Posthumanism: Secular Notion of Transcendence and Its Metaphysical Presuppositions. *Angelicum*, 100(3): 389–417.

Tabaczek, Mariusz (2023c). *Theistic Evolution: A Contemporary Aristotelian-Thomistic Perspective*. Cambridge: Cambridge University Press.

Tabaczek, Mariusz (2024). Vacuum Genesis and Spontaneous Emergence of the Universe from Nothing in Reference to the Classical Notion of Causality and Creation ex nihilo. *Theology and Science*, 22(3): 485–508.

Tabaczek, Mariusz and Michael Chaberek (2024). Theistic Evolution: An Exchange between Mariusz Tabaczek and Michael Chaberek. *Nova et Vetera*, 22(1): 221–284.

Tanzella-Nitti, Giuseppe (2022). *Scientific Perspectives in Fundamental Theology: Understanding Christian Faith in the Age of Scientific Reason*. Claremont, CA: Claremont Press.

Tanzella-Nitti, Giuseppe (2023). Tommaso d'Aquino e il pensiero scientifico contemporáneo. Serge-Thomas Bonino and Luca Tuninetti, eds., *Vetera Novis Augere. Le risorse della tradizione tomista nel contesto attuale. I. Bilancio e prospettive*. Rome: Urbaniana University Press, 151–179.

Thompson, Christopher J. (2017). *The Joyful Mystery: Field Notes toward a Green Thomism*. Steubenville, OH: Emmaus Road.

Thonnard, François-Joseph (1950). *Précis de philosophie*. Paris: Desclée.

Tonquédec, Joseph de (1918). *Une preuve facile de l'existence de Dieu: l'ordre du monde*. Paris: Beauchesne.

Torrell, Jean-Pierre (2003). Situation actuelle des études thomistes. *Recherches de Science Religieuse*, 91: 343–371.

Urráburu, Juan José (1892). *Institutiones Philosophicae. Vol. III: Cosmologia*. Paris: Lethielleux, Rome: Melandri.

Urráburu, Juan José (1896). *Institutiones Philosophicae. Vol. IV: Psychologiae*. Paris: Lethielleux, Rome: Melandri.

Van Riel, Gerd (2022). The History of the Higher Institute of Philosophy. Désiré Mercier and the Foundation of the Higher Institute of Philosophy (1879–1906). published at KU Leuven – Institute of Philosophy, https://hiw.kuleuven.be/en/about-us/history-hiw (27 June).

Vollert, Cyril (1961). The Eucharist: Controversy on Transubstantiation. *Theological Studies*, 22(3): 391–425.

Weisheipl, James (1967). Thomism. *New Catholic Encyclopedia, vol. 14*. New York: Mc-Graw-Hill Book.

Acknowledgements

The first idea for this Element came out of a conversation back in 2021 with Andrew Davison, to whom I am grateful for his patience, insightful comments, and continuous encouragement from the beginning of the writing process. An incipient form of the core idea of the Element was first presented at a workshop organised by Leandro de Brasi at the Universidad de la Frontera, Chile, back in early 2022, in which I received some very positive feedback. I presented some of the ideas in this Element, in a more or less developed form, at the University of Helsinki, Pontificia Universidad Católica de Chile, St Patrick's Pontifical University, Pontificia Univerisità S. Tommaso d'Aquino, Universidad Austral, Universidad del Norte Santo Tomás de Aquino, and Universidad Católica de Salta. I am grateful to all the scholars involved in discussions at these venues. I must also thank Simon Kopf and Gonzalo Recio for ongoing discussions on science-engaged Thomism during the past few years; their input can be discovered throughout these pages; Mariusz Tabaczek, Andrew Meszaros, and Francisco O'Reilly, who read early drafts of parts of this manuscript; and my colleagues at Universidad Austral, whose encouragement to my work is unfailing. Finally, special thanks to my wife, whose loving support saw these pages come to light. This Element was written under the auspices of a grant from the John Templeton Foundation at Universidad Austral.

For Esperanza.

Cambridge Elements

Christianity and Science

Andrew Davison
University of Cambridge

Andrew Davison is the Starbridge Associate Professor in Theology and Science at the University of Cambridge. He is Fellow of Corpus Christi College and Dean of the Chapel, and looks after the arts and humanities work of the Leverhulme Centre for Life in the Universe at the University of Cambridge.

Editorial Board

Natalie Carnes, *Baylor University*
Helen de Cruz, *St. Louis University*
Peter Harrison, *University of Queensland*
Sarah Lane Ritchie, *John Templeton Foundation*
Lisa Sideris, *University of California, Santa Barbara*
Jacob Sherman, *California Institute of Integral Studies*
Ignacio Alberto Silva, *Universidad Austral, Argentina*

About the Series

The Elements series on Christianity and Science will offer an authoritative presentation of scholarship in this interdisciplinary field of inquiry. Opening new avenues for study and research, the series will highlight several issues, notably the importance of historical scholarship for understanding the relationship between Christianity and natural science, and the vital role played by philosophy in this field today.

Cambridge Elements

Christianity and Science

Elements in the Series

Eastern Orthodoxy and the Science-Theology Dialogue
Christopher C. Knight

Science-Engaged Theology
John Perry and Joanna Leidenhag

Science Fiction and Christian Theology
Victoria Lorrimar

Christianity and Agroecology
Matthew Philipp Whelan

Thomism and the Natural Sciences
Ignacio Silva

A full series listing is available at: www.cambridge.org/EOCS

Printed by Integrated Books International,
United States of America